SPECIAL EFFECTS

AN INTRODUCTION TO MOVIE MAGIC

Ron Miller

 Twenty-First Century Books • Minneapolis

This book is dedicated to Sommer Browning, who is, herself, a very special effect.

Acknowledgments
Craig Barron of Matte World; Bob Burns; Columbia TriStar Films; The DAVE School; Michael Daleo; Tim Drnec of FXWest; Robert DeVine of Anatomorphex; Dragon Dronet, Wanda Piety and Peter King of Renegade Effects; John R. Ellis; Roger Evans; Ian Failes; Matt Fairclough; Diego Galtieri, http://www.diegogaltieri.com; Mat Irvine; David Mattingly; Scott McInnes; Judith Miller; Matthew Mungle; New Deal Studios; Christophe Pattou; Patricia Scelfo; Robert Skotak; Pieter Swusten; Chris Walas; Stephen C. Wathen; Max Winston (http://www.hunteachother.com); David Urresti Chiu (http://www.uchiustudio.com); and Allen Yamashita. Foreground miniatures on page 76 produced by MovieStuff, Houston, Texas (http://www.moviestuff.tv). Stills are from "Mission: Noun," an educational video by Michael Daleo, producer and director, Wildcatter Productions, Houston, Texas (http://www.wildcatterproductions.com), and "In My Image," a feature film by Scot McPhie (http://www.mango-a-gogo.com/inmyimage/image.htm).

All the images in the book were provided by the author unless noted otherwise.

Twenty-First Century Books
A division of Lerner Publishing Group
241 First Avenue North
Minneapolis, Minnesota 55401 U.S.A.

Website address: www.lernerbooks.com

Library of Congress Cataloging-in-Publication Data

Miller, Ron, 1947–
    Special effects : an introduction to movie magic / by Ron Miller.
        p.   cm.
    Includes bibliographical references and index.
    ISBN-13: 978–0–7613–2918–3 (lib. bdg. : alk. paper)
    ISBN-10: 0–7613–2918–8 (lib. bdg. : alk. paper)
    1. Cinematography—Special effects. 2. Trick cinematography.
    I. Title.
    TR858.M55 2006
    778.5'345—dc22   2005013123

Manufactured in the United States of America
1 2 3 4 5 6 – BP – 11 10 09 08 07 06

CONTENTS

squib
p.44-45

blue screen 84-86

animatronics 37, 48-49

PART ONE
THE HISTORY OF
SPECIAL EFFECTS

CHAPTER ONE

THE MAGIC LANTERN

Special effects are illusions that enable filmmakers to fool their audiences into thinking they have seen buildings blow up, rocket ships fly to other planets, fantastic creatures, or fabulous cities of the future. But movies are themselves a special effect. The illusion of motion is just that: an *illusion*, a trick.

A motion picture is nothing more than a collection of tens of thousands of individual images, or frames, each one a separate photograph. If you were to simply run the film rapidly, all of the frames would blend together in a blur, in the same way that any fast-moving object passes you in a blur. So why do the pictures appear to move when projected onto a screen? Because of an effect of the brain and eye called short-range apparent motion. If a small black dot on a sheet of white paper is suddenly replaced by another black dot offset by a tiny fraction of inch, it will appear to the eye that the original dot *moved* to the new position. This is because the human eye interprets small, rapid changes in position as actual motion.

A motion picture projector does not project a continuous image of the film. The projector is equipped with a shutter that allows only one frame at a time to be projected onto the screen. The difference between one frame and the next is very slight, since there are twenty-four frames for every second of action. When projected at that speed, the quick changes from one frame to another combined with the small change of position of objects and people between frames are

A simple animated cartoon can be created with an ordinary pad of paper.

You will need: A pen or pencil and colored markers; a pad of stiff unlined paper about 4 by 6 inches (10 by 15 cm)

First, decide on some simple action to animate: a spaceship taking off, an athlete jumping over a hurdle, or someone dancing, for example.

Starting with the top sheet of paper in the pad, draw your first picture near the edge so it can easily be seen when the pages are flipped. (You may want to sketch the drawing in pencil first so you can change it later.) Turn to the next page and do your second drawing. As you do so, keep flipping back to the first drawing as a guide. Keep the difference between the drawings small. Do the rest of the drawings in this way— always checking back to the previous one—until your cartoon is completed. Now, by grasping the bound edge of the pad in one hand, flip the pages from front to back and watch your animated cartoon.

Make a drawing on each page of the pad, with each drawing illustrating a slightly different position of your character.

perceived by the eye as actual motion. If the projection speed is slowed down to ten frames a second or less, the eye stops seeing motion and becomes aware of the individual flickering pictures.

This effect was first described by British physician Peter Mark Roget (who later went on to compile *Roget's Thesaurus*) in 1824 and soon afterward inventors created a bewildering number of toys and other devices that took advantage of the phenomenon. Devices with amazing names, such as the *thaumascope, phenakistoscope, zoetrope,* and *praxinoscope,* allowed people to view animated drawings that lasted

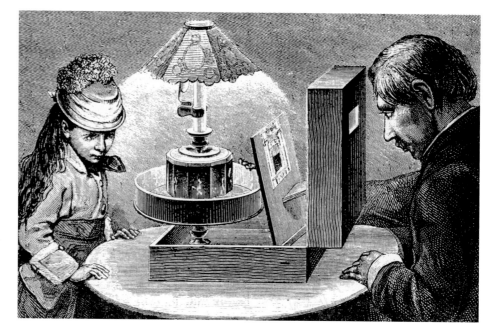

A praxinoscope allowed people to view animated drawings for a second or two.

only a second or two. None of these was a true motion picture, however—at least not as we know it. That didn't happen until the development of two inventions: film sensitive enough to record pictures in a fraction of a second and film on flexible celluloid. (Until the latter part of the nineteenth century, photographs not only required anywhere from several seconds to several minutes to record a scene, they were taken on rigid, fragile glass plates.)

Some of the first experiments in motion pictures used long rolls of paper covered with photographic emulsion, such as the camera invented by Louis Aimé Augustin Le Prince in 1888. To project the image, a powerful light was placed behind the paper strip. This did not create very impressive movies. It was impossible to get paper that was both strong enough to work in a projector and thin enough to allow sufficient light to pass through in order to make a sharp image. When flexible transparent celluloid film was introduced by the Kodak company in 1889, the perfect medium for taking and projecting moving pictures had been found. Thomas Edison and W. K. L. Dickson quickly realized this possibility and invented the first successful, practical motion-picture camera and projector in 1893. However, their device, the kinetoscope, only allowed one person at a time to view a movie. The first successful movies to be shown before an audience were created in France by the Lumière brothers—Auguste and Louis—in 1895. Their films—which lasted only a few

The Lumière brothers created the first publicly shown motion pictures. This is one of their early projectors.

minutes each—were wildly popular. In large part due to the Lumière brothers, motion pictures became big business. It was not long before scores of moviemakers were grinding out hundreds of films every year.

Almost all of the movies made between the 1890s and 1910 were extremely short—ranging from only a few minutes to ten or fifteen minutes at most—the length of a single reel of film. At first, most of these early movies were of commonplace things: trains arriving at stations, street scenes, people working, and so on. The sheer novelty of seeing pictures move was enough for most audiences. But it was not long before moviemakers started telling stories. These were simple at first—little more than mere skits—but they soon began to have real plots using real actors. By the time of World War I (1914–18), many movies were being made at what is now considered to be "feature length"—about ninety minutes. As the films' stories became more complex, so did the process of filmmaking.

CHAPTER TWO

THE ARCHAEOLOGY OF SPECIAL EFFECTS

Special effects are used by moviemakers when it would be too expensive, too dangerous, or outright impossible to film a specific scene. When directors need to shoot in a foreign location but can't afford to go there, or they want to blow up a building or travel to another planet, they call on the special-effects artist. The people who create special effects are often called "movie magicians," which is appropriate since some of the very first special effects ever created for movies were invented by a magician.

THE PIONEERS

Special effects were used onstage long before movies were even invented. It is from these early, live special effects that many of the first movie special effects were developed. Many of these were achieved by ingenious tricks with lighting—such as passing the beam of a spotlight through a prism to create the effect of a rainbow. Lightning could be created by igniting a charge of powdered magnesium, which burns with an intensely bright, white light. Even ghosts could be created by means of a large sheet of plate glass propped up in front of the stage. The reflection of an actor (who was hidden from view) would appear to be transparent, superimposed over the scenery and the actors on the other side of the glass.

By the end of the nineteenth century, there were few effects that could not be re-created onstage: lightning, fire and smoke, floods,

Ghosts were created onstage in nineteenth-century theaters by placing a large sheet of glass at a 45-degree angle to the audience. The reflection of the actor playing the ghost would appear to be superimposed onto the stage. The illustration shows two different ways in which this was done.

The Ghost in the Camera

The actress stands to one side, at 90 degrees from the direction the camera is facing.

A sheet of glass is placed at a 45-degree angle between the background scene and the camera.

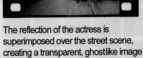

The reflection of the actress is superimposed over the street scene, creating a transparent, ghostlike image.

An effective ghost can be created on film by merely rewinding the film in the camera and reexposing it—an effect called "double exposure." Another way to create a transparent ghost effect is the way the old stage magicians did it. If a sheet of Plexiglas is mounted in front of the camera at an angle of 45 degrees, the camera will record the scene in front of it as well as anything at right angles to the side. An actor standing in front of a black background to the side of the camera will appear superimposed onto the main scene.

A simple piece of clear glass is all that is needed to create a ghostly effect.

earthquakes, and even trips to the Moon were all commonplace illusions. Enormous paintings called "dioramas" and "panoramas" were exhibited in specially built theaters. They re-created sunsets, storms, and the changing of the seasons through the use of clever lighting, projected images, and mechanical effects.

Still photographers in the nineteenth century also developed many of the techniques later used in motion-picture special effects. Double exposures—superimposing one image on another—was a common effect. Sometimes it was used for comical purposes, but occasionally it was used by fraudulent mediums who duped their clients into thinking they were true "spirit photographs" of long-lost loved ones. Another effect developed by photographers was the use of the split screen. One half of a photographic plate was covered with black paper and an exposure was made. Then the black paper was moved to the other half of the plate, which was then exposed again. When the plate was processed, effects such as having someone talking to themselves could be accomplished. This is a technique that was adapted by the earliest filmmakers and is still in use today.

The photographer created this image of a man boxing with himself by using the split screen. For the first exposure, he covered half of his lens with an opaque card. He then covered the other half of the lens with the card for the second exposure.

In 1895 Georges Méliès—a well-known magician in Paris at the time—began making movies employing many of the stage techniques he had learned during his career, as well as many he invented especially for his films. Although today most of his films seem quaint or even crude, they amazed his audiences, who had never before seen anything like them.

Many of the techniques Méliès invented are still in use today. Among them are the substitution shot, stop-motion animation, and double exposure. The substitution shot, which was probably the first cinematic special effect ever created, was invented by accident when Méliès stopped his camera while filming people walking along a sidewalk. After a few minutes he started it again. When he projected the finished film, he was astonished to see people suddenly disappear, replaced by entirely new pedestrians. "I suddenly saw an omnibus changed into a hearse," he wrote in astonishment. Both he and other filmmakers quickly realized that by stopping the camera, rearranging part of a scene, and restarting the camera again, all sorts of amazing effects could be created. It was first used in the movie *The Execution of Mary Queen of Scots* (1895). In this film, the camera was stopped and the actors held their positions just as the ax was poised to fall on the queen. A dummy was then substituted for the actress, and the camera was restarted to create the illusion of the beheading. The substitution shot is still used today to make objects suddenly appear and disappear.

Stop-motion animation makes inanimate objects appear to move on their own. The technique is similar to making an animated cartoon, except that three-dimensional objects are used instead of drawings. For instance, to make a puppet appear to be alive, it is moved incrementally through a range of motions and photographed one frame at a time with each change of position. When the film scene is run at the conventional film speed of twenty-four frames per second, the illusion is created that the creature is moving. Edwin Porter made one of the first all stop-motion films in 1906 called *The Teddy Bears*. The short sequence of frolicking teddy bears, which lasts just over one minute, took approximately fifty-six hours to animate.

Double exposures are probably the simplest of all effects to accomplish. All the filmmaker needs to do is shoot a scene, rewind the film in the camera, and shoot something different. Transparent ghost effects are easily accomplished this way. If a strip of film

Georges Méliès was a stage magician who used his talents for illusion to create marvelous motion pictures filled with fantastic scenes.

He carefully studied the technology, and then had projectors, printers, and other equipment custom-made to his own designs.

Méliès soon began using his camera to document acts on the stage of the Theatre Robert-Houdin. By the end of 1896, Méliès had begun combining his knowl-

Georges Méliès (born Marie-Georges-Jean Méliès in 1861) was a successful magician who owned a theater built by the famous magician Robert-Houdin. After seeing his first movie in 1895, Méliès purchased a motion-picture camera and began making his own films.

Below (left) is a sketch Méliès drew of a scene he wanted to film showing a man blowing up a head like a balloon. Below (right) is the scene as filmed. Méliès used double exposure to achieve this effect. The head was superimposed over the original scene. The black background kept the audience from noticing that it was transparent.

makes more than two passes through the camera, the result is a multiple exposure.

Edwin Porter was also responsible for *The Great Train Robbery* (1903), a twelve-minute film that was one of the first to tell a story. It featured an in-camera matte effect—one of the very first ever attempted—in which the image of a passing train was inserted edge of magic with filmmaking to produce the first "trick" films. These first simple films relied on double exposures to create the illusion of people and objects appearing and disappearing at will or changing from one form to another.

Like most films of this time, Méliès's were very short—only a few minutes in length. His best-known film, *A Trip to the Moon* (1902), was the longest (over twenty minutes) and one of the most complex films he ever made. It employed every trick he had learned or invented. Even today, the film seems amazing. It was based on the novel *From the Earth to the Moon*, and it is said that the book's famous author, Jules Verne, visited the set during the filming.

Because of the lack of international copyright laws, Méliès's films were widely pirated, and although millions of people saw them, he did not make very much money from them. On the other hand, other filmmakers learned from what Méliès had created and not only used his effects techniques in their own films, but also began improving on them. Even today, many of the techniques Méliès invented are still being used in one form or another. Although Méliès made over five hundred films, he made only a handful after *A Trip to the Moon* and died poor and nearly forgot.

Méliès's spaceship makes a messy touchdown on the moon in his 1902 epic.

into a window. Porter accomplished this by first filming the scene with the window blacked out. He then rewound the film and shot the passing train, but this time using a countermatte in front of the camera that blacked out everything *except* the window. When the film was processed and projected, the train appeared to be outside the window. Today the matte looks a little shaky, because it

Other filmmakers tried to achieve more realistic effects than Méliès. Here a train wreck is created in a film by R. W. Paul. This appeared very realistic to audiences of the time.

was difficult to maintain perfect registration with the early cameras that were available when the film was made, but the effect is still very realistic.

Other early pioneers of trick motion-picture photography were R. W. Paul, who, between 1901 and 1910, made a great many short films that rivaled those of Mèliés and G. A. Smith. One of Smith's films, *The Airship Destroyer* (1909), was an ambitious effort that depicted the bombing of London by enemy dirigibles. Although most of Paul's films were wild fantasies similar to those of Mèliés, one of his short films, *Railway Collision* (1898), featured the first attempt to realistically re-create a disaster by means of miniatures.

As both motion pictures and their audiences became more sophisticated, special effects had to become much more realistic if there was any hope of them being believable. Many new techniques and inventions were developed to increase the realism of special effects. One of the very earliest techniques is still used today. This is the matte painting.

Perfected in 1907 by Norman O. Dawn, matte paintings allowed directors to save money by only building a portion of a set and filling in the rest with a painting. To accomplish this, Dawn placed a

Matte paintings can be used to complete sets. In this example from The Fountainhead, *a ceiling was added by matte artist Chesley Bonestell. This not only saved a great deal of money, but allowed the director to place lights and sound equipment directly above the set in the area later covered by the matte painting.*

large sheet of plate glass in front of the camera. He then painted onto the glass that portion of the scene that needed to be replaced, leaving the rest clear. For example, only the gate and part of the wall of a castle needed to be constructed. The rest of the castle would be painted onto the glass. When the camera shot through the glass, the painted scene appeared superimposed over the real-life scene. Although digital matte painting has today almost entirely replaced glass painting, the traditional technique is still occasionally used.

SPECIAL EFFECTS BECOME A SPECIALTY

By the 1920s, the major U.S. and European film studios had established special departments devoted to creating what were then called "trick shots" (the term "special effects" was not widely used until 1926) to accommodate the increasing demand for visual and mechanical effects. The effects department was considered one of the most important parts of a studio because it enabled the studio to save money.

It was becoming harder to fool audiences into accepting the crude effects of earlier films. Filmmakers had to find more sophisticated ways to make their movies appear realistic. An invention that went a long way toward achieving this was the traveling matte. It was a system invented in 1916 by Frank Williams that allowed actors photographed against a special monochromatic (single-color) background to be combined with an entirely different background. This technique is related to double exposure, but resolves one of the main drawbacks of the double exposure. In a normal double exposure, the superimposed figures are transparent and ghostlike. This is good if the director wants to depict a ghost, but bad if he wants the person or object to appear solid. The traveling matte allowed the superimposed objects to have a much more realistic appearance. Williams's process was successful—it was used in such landmark silent films as *Ben-Hur* (1925) and *The Lost World* (1925)—but it also had many drawbacks that later traveling matte systems resolved.

One of the first great geniuses of movie special effects was Willis O'Brien (1886–1962). His specialty was stop-motion animation, to which he brought a sense of reality no one had ever before achieved. O'Brien's animated animals and other creatures seemed incredibly lifelike. When scenes from *The Lost World* (1925) were shown at a meeting of scientists, many of them believed they were looking at film of real, living dinosaurs!

Willis O'Brien set new standards for realism in the effects he created for The Lost World. His animated dinosaurs appeared so lifelike that they fooled some scientists.

One of O'Brien's great talents was the ability to give his creatures real personalities. O'Brien created the special effects for *King Kong* (1933), which has become one of the great classics, not only of special-effects cinema but of the history of motion pictures. O'Brien later did the animation for *Son of Kong* (1933), *Mighty Joe Young* (1949), and other films. One that is especially worthy of mention is *The Last Days of Pompeii* (1935), for which OBie (as he was known to his friends) provided the climactic spectacle of the destruction of the title city by a volcanic eruption. Although the film did not feature his trademark animation, it did feature spectacular matte paintings, miniatures, and rear projection. The latter is a technique that allowed actors to be placed into miniature landscapes by installing tiny translucent screens into the scenery. When film was projected onto the backs of the screens, the actors in it appeared to be within the miniature scenery. The edges of the screens were disguised by plants and rocks so the deception was very effective.

Stop-motion animation pioneer Willis O'Brien is seen here animating a scene from Mighty Joe Young. (Photo courtesy of Bob Burns)

In Mighty Joe Young, live action elements such as the lion in the cage were inserted by rear projection.

As motion pictures became more elaborate and more spectacular, so did special effects. The small, crude cardboard model buildings that satisfied audiences at the turn of the century had grown into the vast, elaborate plaster cities created for films such as *Metropolis* (1926) and *Just Imagine* (1930). In the latter, a model of New York in 1980 (still fifty years in the future when the film was made) filled an entire aircraft hangar. Created by 205 engineers and craftsmen over a period of five months, it was equipped with broad freeways holding hundreds of moving cars. In *Deluge* (1933), New York City was completely destroyed by earthquake and tidal wave. For this film, a model of the city was built on a huge platform 100 feet (30 m) on each side. It had buildings up to 12 feet (3.7 m) tall made of thin plaster shells. By placing sections of the platform on movable rollers, the devastating effects of an earthquake could be simulated. Later, huge dump tanks were used to inundate the wrecked city in a vast tidal wave. This sequence was so effective that it was later reused in several other movies.

One of the largest miniature cities ever constructed for a film was built for Just Imagine. *It was so large it filled an entire aircraft hangar.*

The model of New York created for the film Deluge *was enormous. Made of thin plaster and set on movable platforms, the buildings crumbled realistically in this early disaster film.*

The Shüfftan Process

One of the problems that faced early special-effects designers was that of inserting live actors into miniature sets. One very successful solution was developed by German cameraman Eugen Shüfftan (later called Eugene Shuftan). In his method, the camera faced a mirror that reflected the image of the model building. The reflective surface of the mirror was then carefully scraped away from just that part that reflected the door or window in which the actor was to appear. This left an area of clear glass. If the actor was then positioned on the other side of the mirror, at just the right distance that she filled the clear area and looked the right size, she would appear to be standing in the door or window of the miniature building. Fritz Lang used this for the scene in *Siegfried* (1924) where a group of dwarves is changed into stone. His most extensive use of the technique was in *Metropolis* (1926), where it was used to insert crowds of people into miniatures of the future city. The Shüfftan process was used in many other films of the time, such as *Things to Come* (1936), and even as recently as *Aliens* (1986).

By using mirrors, the Shüfftan process allows live action to be inserted into a miniature set.

The reflection of the actress is superimposed over the model by the mirror

The actress is positioned as far from the mirror as needed in order to appear to be the right size

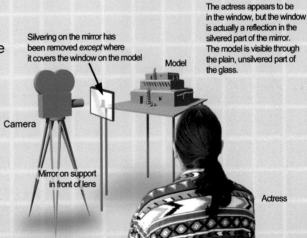

Silvering on the mirror has been removed *except* where it covers the window on the model

The actress appears to be in the window, but the window is actually a reflection in the silvered part of the mirror. The model is visible through the plain, unsilvered part of the glass.

Model

Camera

Mirror on support in front of lens

Actress

Meanwhile, European studios—especially those in Germany—were evolving special effects into a fine art. UFA, the largest film studio in Germany, created numerous films containing groundbreaking special effects that influenced films made both in Europe and the United States for decades. In 1924, director Fritz Lang made *Die Nibelungen*, a two-part film based on the same German legends that had inspired Richard Wagner's great opera series, *The Ring of the Nibelung*. A special-effects highlight was the creation of the enormous fire-breathing dragon, Fafnir, a 50-foot (15-m) creation that required seventeen technicians to operate it. Lang went on to create other milestone special-effects films. The most significant of these was *Metropolis* (1926), which used virtually every state-of-the-art special-effects technique available at the time. It was enormously influential, inspiring films made even as recently as *Blade Runner* (1982).

THE 1930S AND 1940S

The special-effects technique that probably reached the highest level of development during the 1930s and 1940s was the matte painting. Motion pictures such as *The Wizard of Oz* (1939), *Gone With the Wind* (1939), *The Thief of Bagdad* (1940), and *Citizen Kane* (1941) depended heavily on the matte artist for believable re-creations of the fantasy worlds of Oz, the South during the Civil War, ancient Persia, and New York of the 1890s. The introduction of color film made the work of matte artists more difficult while at the same time allowing them to achieve greater reality. Chesley

Everything in this scene from the classic film Citizen Kane is a painting, with the sole exception of the tiny figure of the actor in the distance. The effect was achieved by first shooting the scene with everything but the actor blacked out with a stationary matte (top). A Chesley Bonestell painting was then shot with a black area in the center (middle). When the two pieces of film were combined, the illusion of the actor standing at the end of a long hall was the result (bottom). Notice that even the reflection of the actor in the polished floor was added by the artist.

Matte painter Chesley Bonestell created this dizzying scene for the comedy The Horn Blows at Midnight.

Bonestell (1888–1986) was the highest-paid matte artist of his time, and his paintings were extraordinarily effective, often incorporating animated elements within the artwork to help "bring them to life." For instance, a painting Bonestell created for *The Horn Blows at Midnight* (1945), which showed a dizzying view from a skyscraper of the streets below, included moving cars with headlights. His spectacular panoramic painting for *The Adventures of Mark Twain* (1944) had moving figures in a crowd, created by subtly shifting paper cutouts of real actors. For *The Hunchback of Notre Dame* (1939), Bonestell re-created Notre Dame Cathedral and medieval Paris.

Animator Marcel Delgado takes a look at the unfinished King Kong stop-motion animation puppet. (Photo courtesy of Bob Burns)

While the movie *King Kong* (1933) is rightly most famous for the amazing stop-motion animation work of Willis O'Brien, much of Kong's realism came from the meticulous miniature sets and matte paintings—done primarily by Mario Larrinaga—that created the world in which he lived. By shooting through layers of painted glass, each with a different element of the scene, a tremendous sense of atmospheric depth was achieved.

One of the great effects pioneers to have begun his career during this period was Linwood G. Dunn (1904–99), often considered the "father of optical printing." This is the method by which different film elements are combined into a single frame. For instance, when doing a simple double exposure, the strip of film containing the actor is one element, and the film containing the background is the second element. The optical printer that Dunn invented was capable of accurately combining a great many elements—all shot at different times. Dunn's processes were essential to the success of such works as *King Kong, Citizen Kane,* and the *Star Trek* television series (1966–69).

The 1930s also saw the beginning of the great cycle of Universal Studios's monster films, which brought imaginative new concepts in both special effects and makeup. Movies such as *Frankenstein* (1931) and *The Wolf Man* (1941) created images that still impress viewers today. Much of the credit is due to pioneering makeup artist Jack Pierce (1889–1968). It took six hours for Pierce to apply the heavy makeup for *Frankenstein* to actor Boris Karloff, which had to be built up layer by layer using dangerous and sometimes toxic materials. It was later in the 1930s that makeup artists developed foam latex appliances, so that ears, noses, chins, and other body parts could be created in molds and later applied to the actor's face with adhesives. Makeup artist Jack Dawn was one of the first to use foam latex makeup in a major film when he helped create characters such as the Cowardly Lion and the Scarecrow for *The Wizard of Oz.*

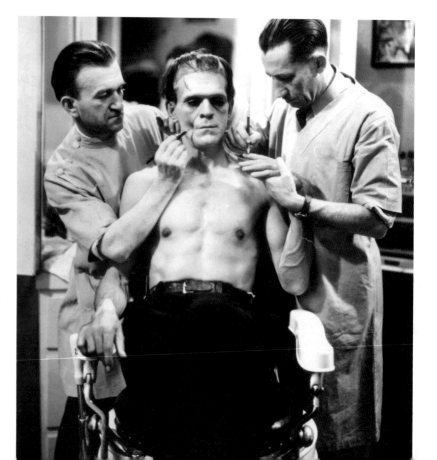

Special-effects makeup wizard Jack Pierce (left) is seen here applying makeup to actor Boris Karloff for his title role in Frankenstein. (Photo courtesy of Bob Burns)

One of Universal's series of horror films was a special-effects masterpiece even though its "monster" was only on screen for a few seconds at the very end. *The Invisible Man* (1933) showcased the work of John P. Fulton (1902–65), who combined live physical effects with traveling-matte photography to convincingly create the illusion of a real invisible man.

One of the special-effects landmarks of the 1940s was Britain's fabulous *Thief of Bagdad* (1940). Designed by William Cameron Menzies (1896–1956)—who also created the futuristic cities and machines of another effects masterpiece, *Things to Come* (1936)—*The Thief of Bagdad* was one of the most elaborate, costly fantasy

The Thief of Bagdad was rich in special effects, ranging from traveling mattes to detailed miniatures. Here, invisible wires support a flying carpet as it soars over the heads of amazed spectators, and an enormous genie looms over the entrance to an ancient temple. (Photos courtesy of Bob Burns)

films made until that time. The movie features wonders such as a six-armed mechanical assassin, a genie made to appear 200 feet (61 m) tall by means of traveling matte photography, and a flying horse.

It might seem strange to think that a lighthearted fantasy film would have been produced in Nazi Germany during the height of World War II, but *Münchhausen* (1943)—a movie based on the famous story by R. E. Raspe about a fabulous, tall-tale-telling nobleman—was a color extravaganza on a scale with England's *The Thief of Bagdad*. It featured numerous beautifully realized special effects that ranged from an oil painting that comes to life, to Baron Münchhausen riding a speeding cannonball, to a balloon trip to the Moon.

During and immediately after World War II, the demand for realistic re-creations of battle scenes also pushed the art of miniatures to new heights. Films such as *Five Seconds Over Tokyo* (1944), *The Dam Busters* (1955), and *The Bridges of Toko-Ri* (1955) contained special-effects sequences that were astonishing in their scale and realism.

THE 1950s

The studio system collapsed in the 1950s. Until then, a major film studio could control everything about the making of a film: the actors, writers, directors, set design and construction, special effects,

Special-effects technicians are setting up a shot of the flying saucer from This Island Earth. *Instead of moving the saucer, the camera is mounted to a metal rod turned by a motor. As the rod turns, the camera is moved smoothly in one direction or the other. This created the effect of the saucer moving smoothly through space, avoiding the jiggling and bouncing of a model hanging from wires. (Photo courtesy of Bob Burns)*

Technicians prepare the miniature saucer for its landing on the planet Metaluna in This Island Earth. *The size of the model and set is revealed in this shot. (Photo courtesy of Bob Burns)*

everything involved in the production of a movie could be found within the studio walls. Many of the studios even owned the theaters that showed the finished movies. In 1950 the Supreme Court declared that this practice was monopolistic and ordered the studios to sell their theaters. The big film studios, such as MGM, Paramount, and Warner Brothers, could no longer afford to maintain their own special-effects departments. Many of the special-effects technicians started their own facilities, providing special effects as independent contractors to whatever studio hired them. Also at about this same time, independent filmmakers began making movies outside the big studio environment. Since the independents did not have their own studios, they depended on the freelance special-effects houses.

Special-effects technicians found plenty of work in the scores of science-fiction films that were made during the 1950s. While a few of these were class projects that had the backing of a major studio, by far the majority were produced by independent "poverty row" companies operating on shoestring budgets. They were in large part responsible for the seemingly endless string of movies about giant insects, mutated monsters, and alien invaders. The special effects for these films ranged from terrible, which unfortunately describes the vast majority of them, to superb, such as those for *Them!* (1954), *This Island Earth* (1955), and *Earth vs. the*

One of the full-size mechanical ants from the Academy Award-nominated monster movie, Them! *(Photo courtesy of Bob Burns)*

Flying Saucers (1956). In fact, the special effects for *Them!*, a movie about giant ants invading Los Angeles, were nominated for an Academy Award.

Some of the science-fiction movies of the 1950s are landmark science-fiction films—films that not only employed state-of-the-art special effects but were also very good movies. One of the first of these was *Destination Moon* (1950), created by producer George Pal

Howard and Theodore Lydecker

The brothers Howard (1911–69) and Theodore (1908–90) Lydecker were responsible for the spectacular special effects in the movie serials made by Republic Pictures from the 1930s to the 1950s. They specialized in creating extremely realistic effects on very low budgets. Among the qualities that made their effects so believable were meticulously constructed models and an insistence that their effects be created "in camera." That means that they were achieved during the original filming, without resorting to traveling mattes or other optical work. Because the effects were shot simultaneously on the same film stock, the image quality was very high. The Lydeckers developed a technique for flying model aircraft (and even people, such as the rocket-powered Commando Cody) that produced very realistic results. The "Lydecker Technique" gave complete control over the movement of the aircraft and is still used today.

Theodore (wearing glasses) and Howard Lydecker, the special-effects masters responsible for the incredible effects seen in scores of serials and feature films (Photos courtesy of Bob Burns)

(1908–80), who went on to produce and sometimes direct several other important effects films. Pal had begun his career in motion pictures in Europe, creating a series of stop-motion animated short subjects he called "Puppetoons."

Destination Moon was his second full-length live-action feature. It told the story of the first spaceship flight to the Moon, which was depicted so realistically that it inspired many young people to

The large size of one of the Lydeckers' spaceship models can be seen in this photo, as it is being prepared for its flight over the landscape. The man on the left is holding the horizontal wires that will guide the model. (Photos courtesy of Bob Burns)

After Republic Pictures closed in 1959, the Lydeckers worked for Walt Disney and Universal Studios, where they created effects for films such as *The Birds* (1963) and *It's a Mad, Mad, Mad, Mad World* (1963), and television shows such as *Voyage to the Bottom of the Sea* and *Lost in Space*. Many consider their greatest work to have been on *Tora! Tora! Tora!* (1970), a film about the Japanese attack on Pearl Harbor in 1941.

In the first of these two scenes (top) from the old serial adventure Radar Men From the Moon, the model spaceship flies over a real landscape. It appears to be larger than it really is for the simple reason that it is much closer to the camera than the background.

eventually go into careers in astronautics. It rightly received the Academy Award for special effects that year. Pal went on to create other classic science-fiction films such as *War of the Worlds* (1953), which vividly depicted the invasion of Earth by Martians and which also received an Academy Award for its effects.

MGM's *Forbidden Planet* (1956) was a low-budget B movie that grew to A-movie proportions before it was finished, resulting in one of the best-looking and most important science-fiction films to be produced during the 1950s. Telling the story of a rescue mission to a distant planet in the far future, *Forbidden Planet* employed innovative and imaginative art direction, incredible miniatures, cel animation, and matte paintings to create a totally convincing alien world. The most memorable effect in the film was Robbie the Robot, an extraordinarily sophisticated prop that is almost as famous as the movie itself. A major influence on the development of *Star Trek* (1966–69), *Forbidden Planet* remains as watchable today as it was when first released.

Ray Harryhausen (born 1920), who had been Willis O'Brien's assistant on *Mighty Joe Young,* eventually became the acknowledged master of stop-motion animation, creating the effects for such classic science-fiction and fantasy films as *It Came From Beneath the Sea* (1955) and *Twenty Million Miles to Earth* (1957). These were followed by *The Seventh Voyage of Sinbad* (1958), *Jason and the Argonauts* (1963), *Clash of the Titans* (1981), and many others. His first solo film was the

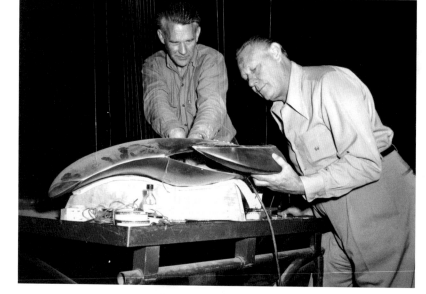

Two technicians are working on one of the Martian war machines for the George Pal production of War of the Worlds. The many fine wires that suspended the model and also provided electricity to its lights and motors can be seen. In the film, these wires were mostly obscured by smoke.

low-budget *Beast From 20,000 Fathoms* (1952). Made for less than $200,000, it generated more than $5 million, thereby setting the stage for the decade of giant monster films to come. For his films, Harryhausen developed a special split-screen technique called "Dynamation" that allowed him to convincingly combine his animated creations with live-action actors. Harryhausen's films are effective not just because of the technical expertise he brought to them, but because of his ability to bring real life to his animated creations, imbuing them with individuality and distinctive personalities. Even though his techniques have been largely superceded by computer-generated digital animation, Harryhausen's films are still the standard for excellence by which 3-D animation is judged.

Not every important special-effects film of this era was science fiction. Director Cecil B. De Mille had a fondness for including spectacular effects sequences in his epic movies, and his masterpiece, *The Ten*

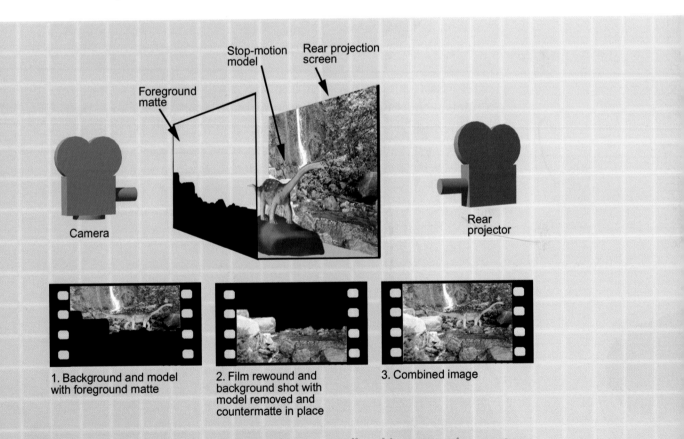

Stop-motion model

Rear projection screen

Foreground matte

Camera

Rear projector

1. Background and model with foreground matte

2. Film rewound and background shot with model removed and countermatte in place

3. Combined image

Dynamation was created by Ray Harryhausen to allow his stop-motion creatures to be inserted into live-action scenes. Because Harryhausen could see the relationship of his model to the projected background, he could make his puppets appear to react realistically with human actors.

Commandments (1956), was no exception. Although the movie is a veritable encyclopedia of special-effects techniques, it is the parting of the Red Sea that stands out as the film's centerpiece. It was one of the most complex and expensive effects ever created, employing everything from traveling mattes to the construction of a miniature waterfall. John P. Fulton won an Academy Award for his astonishing special effects for *The Ten Commandments*, beating out *Forbidden Planet* for the award.

TRIUMPHS AND DISASTERS IN THE 1960S AND 1970S

All other special-effects movies made during the decade of the 1960s are overshadowed by Stanley Kubrick's *2001: A Space Odyssey* (1968). Breaking entirely new ground in effects technology, it achieved levels of realism never seen before. It also helped introduce the new technique of motion control, where a computer-guided motorized camera could precisely replicate the same movement over and over again. *2001* also pioneered the use of front-projection, which provided much more realistic backgrounds than the old rear-projection technique, as well as the slit-scan process responsible for the now-famous "psychedelic" star gate sequence at the end of the film.

To achieve a sense of the vast size of the spacecraft in the film, models were constructed on an unprecedented scale. Where in the past the model for a movie spaceship might be only a few feet long, the model of the *Discovery* in *2001* was 53 feet (16.15 m) long! To record the fine detail with which the models were covered required extreme depth of field—that is, objects very close to the camera lens had to be as sharply focused as objects far away. The only way to achieve this is to "stop" the lens by reducing its iris to the smallest possible opening. This results in great depth of field, but it also requires vast amounts of light since the camera lens is closed to a mere pinhole. Since this means long exposures, the models were actually photographed in stop-motion. The space station, for instance, was made to rotate on a shaft extremely slowly—so slowly that its motion was barely detectable to the eye. Instead of photographing the station continuously, individual frames were shot, using exposures of several seconds each. Since the model was moving during the exposure, this meant that it was blurred very slightly. When the finished film was run at the proper speed of twenty-four frames a second, the slight blurring of each frame helped make the motion of the station look very realistic, avoiding the jerky, hard-edged look of traditional stop-motion animation. This was a very early application of the more complex "Go-Motion" technique refined and perfected by Phil Tippett and Dennis Muren in shooting the stop-motion tauntaun creature in *The Empire Strikes Back* (1980).

Where the 1950s had seen a spate of science-fiction and monster movies, the theme of the 1970s was disaster films. Beginning with effects-laden spectacles such as *Airport* (1970) and *The Poseidon Adventure* (1972), Hollywood studios began a competition to see which could outdo the other in the scale of the catastrophes they brought to the screen. While not great films by any means—and some would argue that they are not even good films—the best of them, such as *Earthquake* (1974) and *The Hindenburg* (1975), featured spectacular achievements in special effects. The latter was awarded a special Oscar for its special effects, which had been created by the legendary matte artist Al Whitlock. The disaster movie trend came to an end with *Meteor* (1979), a disaster itself that was sunk by its mediocre and unbelievable special effects.

However, just as *The Ten Commandments* defined the state of the art of special effects of the 1950s, and *2001* that of the effects of the 1960s, the 1970s is surely the decade of *Star Wars* (1977). Not only was the film itself a blockbuster, it made stars of the special-effects artists who helped create it. Industrial Light and Magic, the inde-

The Special Effects Supervisor

By the end of the twentieth century, special effects had become such a complex process that no one person could be capable of creating the effects for a film. Instead, several people, each practicing their own specialty, worked under the supervision of an overall director of effects, called the "effects supervisor."

As effects supervisor Mat Irvine explains, "If you split effects work down into its overall types, you'll get models and miniatures, special props, floor effects, special make-up/sculpture/creature effects, and—these days—CGI. One person cannot be expected to be an expert in actually doing all of this. Most of these specialties need dedicated people working full time just to keep up with modern techniques. A production company would probably only want to deal with one overall person in creating the effects for a film, hence the need for a 'supervisor.' Having said that, many movies these days have such a heavy FX workload that they may indeed have several 'supervisors,' one for each different aspect."

pendent special-effects company that was created from the team of effects artists who had worked on *Star Wars*, is almost as well known a name today as Warner Brothers, 20th Century Fox, or Paramount. Other effects artists who worked on the film, such as John Dykstra, went on to form their own successful independent companies.

The extraordinary success of *Star Wars* and *Close Encounters of the Third Kind* (1977) opened a floodgate of effects-heavy science-fiction films such as *Superman* (1978) and *Alien* (1979), many of which—in trying to outdo their predecessors in astonishing audiences—introduced brand-new special-effects techniques and technologies. The ever-increasing need for special- effects artists also created a new job market, attracting scores of talented individuals into the field. These artists brought new ideas and innovative techniques with them, creating new special- effects companies to compete with Industrial Light and Magic.

The company Industrial Light and Magic was created from the team of effects artists that worked on the Star Wars movie. For the first time, special-effects creators were stars in their own right and the phrase "special-effects movie" began to describe a particular type of film. (Photos COURTESY OF LUCASFILMS LTD., © 1977 and 1997 Lucasfilm Ltd. & TM. All rights reserved. Used under authorization. Unauthorized duplication is a violation of applicable law.)

CHAPTER THREE

THE **DIGITAL** REVOLUTION

Even though technology allowed traditional effects to be continuously improved—this being especially true of the traveling matte—films made up until the early 1980s all employed special effects that were only variations and improvements of techniques that had been used for generations. It was not until the advent of computer technology that anything totally new was added to the arsenal of the special-effects artist. The computer was more than new: It was revolutionary.

The first film to use computer-generated imagery to any extent was *TRON* (1982)—although some early computer-generated elements were used to a limited degree in *Westworld* (1973) and *Futureworld* (1976). With much of its action taking place in an imaginary world set within a computer, *TRON*'s animation did not have to look very realistic, and it didn't.

In that same year, Paramount released *Star Trek II: The Wrath of Khan* (1982), which featured a single, brief computer-generated sequence in which an entire planet is created in just a few seconds, from barren rock to lush vegetation, lakes, and cloud-filled skies. While lasting only a few seconds on film, the "Genesis effect" was much more realistic than anything attempted in *TRON*. The success of the technique led to *The Last Starfighter* (1984), which was the first film to feature extensive use of computer-generated imagery (or

CGI)—most notably, the use of computer-generated models instead of traditionally constructed ones, such as those used in *2001* or *Star Wars*. Still, while the CGI spacecraft could do things that would be difficult or impossible to accomplish with a model, they did not look nearly as believable, with flat, plasticlike surfaces and little or no texture.

The first computer-generated character (albeit a rather cartoonish one) was the "stained glass knight" featured in *Young Sherlock Holmes* (1985). But directors were still wary of computer-generated special effects even as late as the early 1990s. No one had attempted any large-scale creation of living creatures since it was generally believed that computers were incapable of achieving the believability required. It was one thing to create robots and spaceships, but it was assumed that audiences would be far more critical of a computer-generated human being or animal. Yet, with the intense pressure of studios and special effects companies to outdo one another, along with the influx of computer-savvy talent and the logarithmic advances in computer technology, it was not long before computers became a major tool for special-effects artists, perhaps *the* major tool.

Director Steven Spielberg (born 1946) at first intended to create the dinosaurs of *Jurassic Park* (1993) through a combination of tra-

Using a combination of digital effects and mechanical effects to create realistic dinosaurs, Jurassic Park's special effects team won the 1993 Academy Award for Best Special Effects. (Photo courtesy of © Close Murray/CORBIS SYGMA)

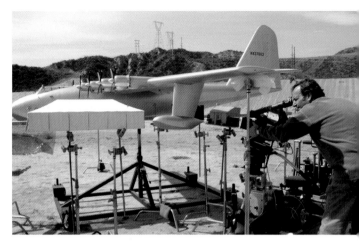

Robert Legato, the special- effects supervisor for The Aviator, checks the setup of the 1/16 scale miniature seaplane to make sure that it is properly aligned with the other elements in the scene.

ditional 3-D animation and animatronics (full-size mechanized models), but tests of computer-generated dinosaurs done by animator Phil Tippett convinced Spielberg to do the majority of the dinosaur effects digitally. This turned out to be a decision that affected the entire course of the special-effects industry. *Jurassic Park* demonstrated that computer-generated effects were not only capable of creating astonishingly realistic images, but could convincingly re-create living creatures as well. The dinosaurs of *Jurassic Park* genuinely seemed to be living, breathing animals.

As important as its ability to *create* images is the computer's capability to *combine* images. In the past, this always involved the combination of images from two or more pieces of film onto one, such as in the creation of traveling mattes. However, each time an image is copied, its quality degrades, much like making a photocopy of a photocopy of a photocopy. (The difference in quality in different parts of a scene would often give away the fact that a special effect was taking place.) Each copy of a film is called a "generation," and it was the goal of every special-effects artist to use film removed

Here we see the hanging miniature of the seaplane from the camera's point of view.

This is the finished shot of the seaplane with digital water added in the foreground and digital matte art filling in details in the background. (Photos courtesy of New Deal Studios)

from the original footage by as few generations as possible. The solution would be to shoot all effects on a single strip of film, ideally using the original live-action footage, but the danger is that if something were to go wrong, the original would be ruined and everything would have to be reshot. This could be extremely expensive and perhaps even impossible. Digital images, on the other hand, can be copied hundreds of times, and each copy will be not only of the same quality as the original but absolutely *identical* to the original. Every element in a computer-composited scene looks as good as the original footage.

The triumphant digital special effects of *Jurassic Park* were followed by ever more amazing special-effects films. In fact, "special-effects film" had begun to enter the language as a description of such effects-heavy movies. Among these were George Lucas's

Digital effects have become essential to today's big special-effects movies, as seen here in this still from Star Wars Episode III: Revenge of the Sith.

The special-effects artists who worked on the Matrix trilogy used a combination of digital effects and traditional effects to achieve the most effective and realistic scenes. (Photo courtesy of © Warner Brothers/Photofest)

Phantom Menace (1999), *Attack of the Clones* (2002), and *Revenge of the Sith* (2005), which featured not only digitally created effects, but digital sets and even digital characters. Because of the emphasis movies such as these placed on their digital effects, many people in the industry thought it might mean the end of traditional special effects. But, according to Craig Barron of Matte World, "Predictions of the time, which prophesied the end of all traditional visual effects, were greatly exaggerated. Makeup, creature costumes, animatronic effects, miniatures, and scale models all remain vital crafts, although every one of those disciplines has been changed by computer technology. . . . [But] computer monitors [have] not altered the irreducible essence at the heart of any creative equation—the inventive mind and talent of the individual artist."

Live action, digital matte paintings, miniatures, and traveling mattes all combined to produce this spectacular scene from Lord of the Rings: The Two Towers. (Photo courtesy of New Line Productions)

Barron appears to have been right. In spite of the emphasis—and perhaps overemphasis—movies such as the *Star Wars* sequels have placed upon digital effects, other films, such as the *Matrix* trilogy (1999–2003) or the *Lord of the Rings* trilogy (2001–03), have shown that traditional effects—even old-fashioned low-tech effects—will always have their place alongside digital effects, each doing what it does best and each complementing the other.

PART TWO
HOW IT'S DONE

CHAPTER FOUR

MECHANICAL EFFECTS

Mechanical, or physical, effects were among the first to be employed by motion-picture makers. These are the effects that are performed in front of the camera during the filming of the rest of the action. These might include rain, wind, fog, snow, waves, explosions, bullet hits, breaking glass, collapsing buildings, and so on. Where the prime motive in other areas of special effects is saving money, one of the prime concerns of mechanical effects is safety. The mechanical effects artist enables the actor to take part in action that would otherwise be extremely dangerous or even deadly—and not only for the actor but for the rest of the film crew as well.

WEATHER

Some of the most common special effects are those related to weather. Creating rain can be as easy as spraying water on a window or as difficult as using fire hoses and powerful pumps to drench a set in hundreds of gallons of water. If the rain is occurring during a storm, huge fans—often powered by aircraft engines—can whip up a tempest in no time. A storm at sea or a flood can be re-created by the use of huge "dump tanks." These can release hundreds of gallons of water all at once, sending huge waves crashing through a set.

Huge fans like this are used to create powerful winds, such as when a storm is being generated. This particular machine is powered by propane, so it can be used on any location. (Photo courtesy of Tim Drnec)

Fog can be created in several ways. Frozen carbon dioxide—more commonly known as "dry ice"—will produce a heavy, ground-hugging mist when dropped into warm water. The spooky fog creeping across the ground in movie cemeteries is produced by dry ice. (Dry ice is easily obtained and easily used, but great care must be taken in handling it. Dry ice is *extremely* cold at −109°F [−78.5°C] and can severely damage bare skin.) Banks of fog are created by means of machines that produce "fog"—actually very fine smoke—by heating a special nontoxic oil. By using portable fog makers, special-effects artists can place fog precisely where it is needed.

All special-effects technicians have their favorite recipe for snow. A great many materials have been used since the invention of movies, but potential environmental damage is now an important consideration since artificial snow is usually applied to a large area of a landscape. Today, most movie snow is actually shredded paper. To show snow falling, the paper is put into large overhead hoppers where it is shaken through a coarse screen. If it is not possible to erect overhead supports, the snow may be blown into the air by fans. Background snow is usually a nontoxic foam sprayed from large hoses.

SAFE FIGHTS

When actors get into a fight, they may break bottles over each other's heads, crash into chairs and tables, and get thrown through windows. Since no one wants to really get hurt, this is another area where the special-effects technician steps in. The glass bottles and windows are actually made of a specially made, fragile resin. This breaks easily and does not form dangerous, sharp shards. The special-effects artist can create any kind of glass object and in any color. Chairs and tables are made of lightweight wood—such as balsa or basswood—with preweakened areas that will break under the slightest impact.

PYROTECHNICS

Some special effects are extremely hazardous, even when they are themselves meant to take the place of dangerous actions and stunts. The most dangerous of these are effects involving pyrotechnics: the art of handling fire and explosives.

The most obvious use of explosives in films is in action movies, where gunfire and bullets striking their targets are an important ingredient. Even though movie guns fire blank cartridges—that is, a cartridge that uses a small piece of cardboard instead of a lead bullet—they can still be very dangerous if not used properly. Many people have been injured by guns firing blanks or by using prop guns incorrectly. The actor Brandon Lee died as the result of untrained personnel handling the firearms during the filming of a scene in *The Crow* (1994). For this reason, specially trained and licensed special-effects technicians known as armorers handle everything concerning firearms—including training the actors in the safe handling of the weapons.

Other technicians reproduce the impact of the fake bullets that are fired by the actors. To simulate the impact of bullets on walls, cars, and other objects, bullet holes are created beforehand. If a bullet is meant to hit a door, the technician digs out a chunk of wood. Carefully saving the splinter, he then drills a hole into which he inserts a small explosive device called a squib that can be fired electrically. Replacing the splinter, the technician carefully hides all signs of it so that the wood looks exactly as it did before. To simulate the impact of the bullet, the squib is detonated, blowing off the chunk of wood and realistically creating the impression of a real bullet impact. Bullets blowing holes in trees, car doors, and other objects are created in a similar way.

Compressed air can be used to safely simulate the effects of squibs. A flexible vinyl tube—such as can be found in aquarium supply shops—can be attached to a can of Dust-Off compressed air. The other end of the tube can be hidden in clothing, props, or scenery. The jet of air can then be used to propel dust, stage blood, or any other materials placed in the end of the tube. This is a relatively safe technique that has been used for years by professional effects technicians, although great care must still be taken since materials can be ejected from the tube very quickly. Another technique for safely faking bullet wounds is to use a monofilament fishing line to pull off makeup to reveal an underlying injury.

The same technique is used to show bullets hitting people, though great care has to be taken since squibs can be very dangerous. Usually a small metal plate is placed between the squib and the actor's body. When fired by the technician, the explosion will blow a hole in the actor's clothing. If a small plastic bag of stage blood is placed over the squib, the bullet hit can be made to look even more gruesome.

In re-creating explosions, the primary trick of the special-effects explosives expert is to make an explosion look much larger than it really is. There are a couple of reasons for this, the primary one being safety. A small explosion is less likely to cause real damage or injury than a big one—although the explosives experts take enormous care no matter how large the explosion is going to be. They know that all explosives are extremely dangerous.

Miniatures that are to be blown up—such as the White House or Empire State Building in *Independence Day* (1996)—are carefully constructed with preweakened materials so that the explosives can easily demolish it in a predictable way. The model may also contain special substances that will create balls of flame, smoke, sparks, or whatever else might enhance the final effect. This way the pyrotechnician can achieve the appearance of a big explosion while using the minimum amount of explosives.

For an explosion in the ground, such as might be used in a war film to suggest the impact of a bomb or missile, a hole is dug where the explosion is to occur. A small explosive device called a mortar is

The special-effects crew of Chronicles of Riddick (2004) uses a forklift to shift the 1/5 scale buildings of Helion City. The sequence showing a spaceship that crashes into a city street was shot outdoors at night. The gray area in the middle of the street was specially made to break away under the impact of the spaceship.

Special-effects technicians Jon M. Warren and John Hoffman work on the scale model of the spaceship that will crash.

This sequence shows the three stages in the flaming crash of the spaceship. (Photos courtesy of New Deal Studios)

placed in the hole. This is a kind of small cannon or gun shaped like a squat metal canister containing a carefully measured quantity of black powder. Placed above this is material meant to suggest rocks and other debris thrown by the force of the explosion. These "rocks" are usually pieces of lightweight materials such as cork or Styrofoam. A huge cloud of dust—which helps make the explosion look larger than it really is—can be enhanced by pouring fuller's earth (a finely powdered mineral normally used to clean up oil spills) into the hole. Finally, depending on the needs of the director, other materials can be placed over the mortar. A bag of gasoline, for instance, will produce a huge ball of flame, while other materials will create showers of sparks.

An exploding cake was created safely for MTV's "Buzzkill" series by not using any explosives. Instead, an air cannon was placed beneath the table. The blast of air it released sent the cake flying in all directions. (Photo courtesy of Anatomorphex)

When explosives are buried in a movie set—whether as bullet hits in walls or bombs in the ground—great care is taken to choreograph the movements of the actors so that no one ever gets too close to a detonation. The location of every explosive device is also carefully marked so that they are visible to the people working on the film but cannot be seen by the camera.

Sometimes when just the effect of an explosion is required, an air cannon or an air mortar may be used. This is a device that releases an instantaneous blast of air that can blow huge fountains of water into the air, shatter preweakened sets or miniatures, or cause similar effects when an actual explosive might be too dangerous.

MONSTERS AND ANIMATRONICS

Straddling the border between physical effects and special-effects makeup are animals and creatures that are either worn by actors or are operated entirely by puppeteers. The 1950s were rife with monsters that were little more than actors in rubber suits, a famous example of which is *Godzilla*, which first appeared on screen in 1954 and was quickly followed by dozens of sequels. More often than not, the monsters in these movies looked just like what they were: men in rubber suits. But sometimes these worked very well, such as in *The Creature From the Black Lagoon* (1954), whose gill man is one of the best-realized and most famous of all movie monsters. Even today, in an age of computer-generated creatures, some of the most effective are played by actors in elaborate suits, such as in *Alien* (1979) and *Predator* (1987).

Mechanically operated creatures are called animatronics, a word coined by Walt Disney engineers (or "imagineers" as they call themselves) to describe the extraordinarily lifelike robotic replica of Abraham Lincoln installed for a show at Disneyland. Where the original Disney animatronic characters were operated entirely by computers, most animatronic creatures seen in movies are operated by puppeteers. This is usually done by means of long, flexible cables connected to levers. But in some cases, especially when the creature

A running rhinoceros was required for a television commercial, so special-effects expert Robert DeVine devised this mechanical model that copied the motion of the real animal perfectly.

Once covered with a carefully painted latex skin, the rhinoceros could not be distinguished from a real one. (Photos courtesy of Anatomorphex)

has to move around a lot and cables might be visible or too clumsy to use, the motions are created by small motors hidden within the creature. These motors can then be controlled remotely by radio, like a radio-controlled car or airplane.

Animatronics have been used to create scores of movie monsters, from the dinosaurs seen close-up in *Jurassic Park* to the fearsome queen alien in *Aliens* (1986) to mummies in *The Mummy* (1999). Animatronic characters can become so complex that a dozen or more individual puppeteers are required to operate them. Actors in rubber suits and animatronics are combined when a creature worn by an actor is required to make facial expressions or other special movements that might be controlled remotely by puppeteers.

When it is impossible for a creature to be portrayed by an actor wearing a suit or makeup, it will often be performed by puppeteers. This was necessary in Gremlins (1984) because of the small size of the creatures. In order to create the wide variety of facial expressions, the individual puppets became extremely complex mechanisms with several puppeteers required to operate the "actors" remotely. In some scenes, such as the one set in the movie theater above, a huge number of puppeteers were necessary. (Photos courtesy of Chris Walas)

CHAPTER FIVE

MINIATURES

One of the oldest special-effects techniques is the use of models as stand-ins for full-size objects. They have been in use since the very first movies were made. Miniatures allow the director to create places and things that may not exist or would be too expensive to construct full-size. It would be impractical, for instance, to build a full-size ship in order to film it sinking, or to construct an entire building for a scene in which it burns to the ground. Not only would such things be prohibitively expensive—not to say dangerous—what if something goes wrong and the scene has to be done over? And what if the script calls for something utterly impossible to film "for real," such as a spaceship landing on another planet?

FACING PAGE: *The construction of a special-effects miniature often requires many weeks of work by a large crew of expert model makers, technicians, and craftspeople. (1) The model of the XF-11 airplane for* **The Aviator** *began with its fuselage being carved out of foam.*
(2) After a plastic mold was cast from the foam, details such as rivets were added. (3) Meanwhile, other model makers created the wings, landing gear, and other parts (in the background another miniature airplane is under construction). (4) As the pieces came together, the miniature began to look more like a real airplane, especially once it had been painted. (5) The finished miniature, sitting outdoors on a real runway, is indistinguishable from the real thing. (Photos Courtesy of New Deal Studios)

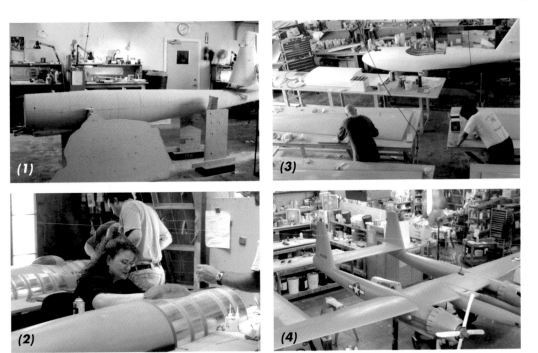

Miniatures not only allow directors to save a lot of money, it gives them a lot more control on their sets since they are working with objects that were specially constructed for their purposes.

Miniatures are usually scale models, which means that they are built to an exact proportion to the original object, whether that be a house, an airplane, or a ship. A full-scale or one-to-one model is the same size as the original. A half-scale model is half the size of the original, a quarter-scale model is one-fourth the size, and so on. There are several ways of indicating the scale, all of which mean the same thing. Scale can be written as a fraction, such as 1/16, meaning that the model is one-sixteenth the size of the original object, or it can be written as a ratio, such as 1:16, which means that one unit on the object equals sixteen units on the original, that is, 16 inches on the real thing.

Since models look more realistic when they are large, the word miniature can seem misleading. Some movie miniatures have been enormous. The *Discovery* spaceship in *2001* was 53 feet (16 m) long and the model of the *Titanic* for the 1997 James Cameron epic was 45 feet (13.7 m) long. Some model ships have been so large they could contain an operator to steer them. The house built for *The Amityville Horror* (1979) was built at one-half scale, which means that it was half as large as a real house.

"Miniatures" can sometimes be quite large, since the larger the model is, the more realistic it will appear. The true scale of this house created for The Amityville Horror is revealed by the people standing near it.

If done well, miniatures can be combined with full-size live-action footage without the audience being any the wiser. Much of the success of a model depends, naturally, on the skill of the model builder. But it must also be photographed properly and in the right conditions. One of the reasons that miniatures are built so large is because of the depth of field. If a model is too small, it may not be possible to keep both it and distant objects in focus. An out-of-focus miniature sitting close to the camera will look exactly like what it is: a small model.

Depth of field can be controlled in two ways. One is the size of the aperture—this is the size of the lens opening, equivalent to the

This is the production designer's original sketch (top) and the finished set (bottom), built in 1/5 scale, depicting a canal in Venice for The League of Extraordinary Gentlemen *(2003). (Photos courtesy of New Deal Studios)*

DEPTH OF FIELD

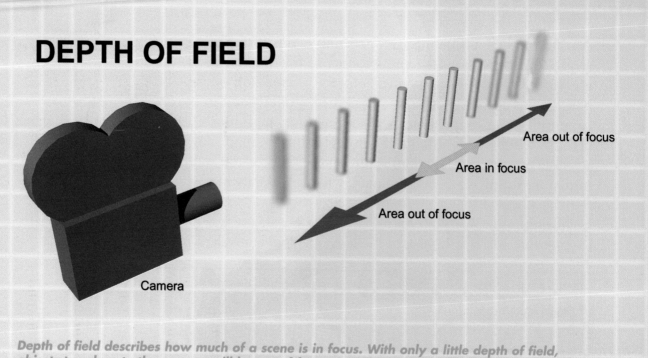

Camera

Area out of focus

Area in focus

Area out of focus

Depth of field describes how much of a scene is in focus. With only a little depth of field, objects too close to the camera will be out of focus, as will objects too far away.

pupil in your eye. A very small aperture results in greater depth of field than a large aperture. Still photos taken with a "pinhole" aperture—which is exactly what it sounds like: an aperture created by pushing a pin though a piece of black paper or aluminum foil—can have everything in focus from the actual front surface of the lens itself to infinity. Because the tiny, pinhole-sized aperture drastically cuts down the amount of light reaching the film, their use requires very long exposures, making them impractical for live-action moviemaking (though they can work very well for stop-action films, where the exposure for each frame can be as long as necessary). Whenever possible, therefore, models are shot with the aperture of the camera set as small as possible, illuminated by extremely bright lights to make up for the reduced amount of light getting through the aperture to the film.

Depth of field is also affected by the type of lens used. Short focal length lenses, such as wide-angle lenses, have more depth of field than long focal length lenses, such as telephoto lenses. So most models are photographed with wide-angle lenses.

Another problem with models is movement. A model does not move the same way as its full-size counterpart. There are three relat-

(1) This is the original sketch created by an art director, showing what the spaceship in the final scene of his movie should look like. (2) Here the model has been constructed and is given its final coat of paint. (3) This is the model in the miniature set, ready for filming. (4) And finally, we see a frame from the finished film. (Photos courtesy of John Ellis)

ed reasons for this: acceleration, weight, and size. Acceleration refers to the fact when something falls it does not fall at a constant rate. Instead, it picks up speed gradually, falling faster and faster until it hits the ground. In fact, there is a very specific formula for calculating the rate of acceleration for something falling under the influence of Earth's gravity: It will fall at the rate of 32 feet per second per second. This simply means that for every second it falls, the object will be falling 32 feet per second faster than during the previous second. In the first second it will be traveling 32 feet per second, 64 feet per second in the next second, 96 feet per second in the third second, and so on. A car plunging off a cliff 150 feet high will hit the ground in just 3 seconds. But a 1/10th scale model car falling off a

Slow motion is used not only to make small objects appear larger, but to emphasize certain scenes for dramatic effect, such as in the *Matrix* series (1999–2003) or *Charlie's Angels* (2000). Slow motion is created by running the film through the camera *faster* than usual. The normal speed for film is twenty-four frames per second. If a ten-second scene is shot at twenty-four frames per second it will last for ten seconds when projected at the same rate, and the action will appear to be normal. If, instead, the same ten-second scene is shot at forty-eight frames a second there will be twice as many frames exposed as before. When projected at twenty-four frames per second, the scene will last twice as long and the action, therefore, will appear to move half as fast. In order to get the slow motion needed to make a model appear realistic, cinematographers will sometimes run film at rates of hundreds of frames per second. Speeded-up action—which is often used for comedic purposes—is achieved in exactly the opposite way: The film is run through the camera slower than normal.

model bridge only 1/10th as high—15 feet—will hit the ground in less than one second. In order to make the fall of the model car believable, its fall has to be slowed down.

Another reason moving models need to be slowed down is that they weigh less in proportion to their full-size counterparts. A model car one tenth as long as a full-size car will not weigh one tenth as much but one hundredth as much, and probably much less since most models are made of lightweight materials, such as plastic and foam. When the model car moves or bounces around, it will look very toylike compared to the movement of a full-size vehicle weighing a ton or more. If a full-size car plunges off a hundred-foot cliff, it will probably be demolished when it hits the ground. The one-tenth model car falling off a ten-foot cliff might only bounce when it hits. Loading the model with lead weights will help this to some degree, but filming in slow motion is the only way to make its movements entirely realistic.

Special effects cinematographers use a rule-of-thumb formula to calculate what film speed to shoot at for different scales of models, although the final choice is determined by what the cinematographer thinks will look best on screen. Often, a miniature scene will be shot simultaneously at different speeds, in order to be able to pick the one that looks most convincing.

If the model has to endure some degree of destruction, then great care has to be taken to make it react just as the full-size object would, so that the model car plunging off the ten-foot cliff will be crushed just as a real car would be. Adding extra weight and making the model of especially fragile materials and prebroken parts will help to make the illusion more convincing.

MINIATURE WATER

Water cannot be miniaturized. This is because of a quality of water called *surface tension.* Molecules of water bond with one another in a way that creates a kind of "skin" on the surface of the water. Unless water is broken up into a fine mist by air pressure or other means, surface tension sets a limit on the size of a drop of water. A rock dropped into a pond creates a splash with drops the same size as those produced by a tidal wave. Therefore, the large drops of water produced by a model immediately reveal the model's small size because the drops will appear too big in comparison to the body of water.

Few things will give away a miniature set faster than seeing a flood with drops of water the apparent size of bowling balls. The best solution is to have water interact with models that are built as large as possible.

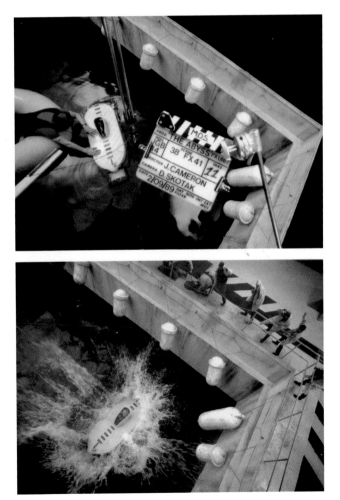

Special-effects expert Bob Skotak set up this miniature shot, showing the launching of a submersible in the film **The Abyss** *(1989). After the miniature was filmed (top) the live-action portion of the scene (bottom) was added around it. (Photos courtesy of Robert Skotak)*

A miniature forest was created by Bob Skotak's team of special effects artists, and then wiped out by a simulated flood for the movie X-Men (2000). (Photos courtesy of Robert Skotak)

But even the huge model of the *Titanic* was not large enough to keep its true size from being revealed when its stern lifted from the water as it sank and oversized drops of water dripped from its propellers. The director could only hope that the audience would be too caught up in the excitement of the scene to notice.

In some films, substitutes for water can be used. Waterfalls can be simulated with marble dust or flour. In an earlier *Titanic* movie—*Raise the Titanic* (1980)—the water seen pouring from the deck of the raised ship is actually salt. Salt was also used for the water seen gushing from a hydrant near the end of *Ghostbusters* (1986). If you look closely at that shot, you will see the salt beginning to pile up around the miniature hydrant just before the scene ends.

Many special-effects scenes are set underwater. In this case, the special-effects technician may decide not to use any water at all. For example, a miniature submarine may be hung by thin wires or monofilament line (the same strong, fine, nearly transparent line used by fishers) within a miniature set. By using rippling lights and a fog or smoke machine to simulate the murkiness of the deep sea, the audience never knows that the scene was actually shot "dry." Doing an effect this way is much easier and cheaper than actually shooting underwater.

In recent years, the use of digital water has been increasing, though there are still some limitations to the believability it can achieve. In *Titanic*, the ocean in which the ship sails was generated digitally, while images of water churning around the bow and the wake left behind were taken from those of a real ship. Nevertheless, some extremely convincing digital water was created for *The Perfect Storm* (2000) and in *Antz* (1996) for the sequence in which the ants' colony is flooded.

CHAPTER SIX

STOP-MOTION ANIMATION

Very early in the history of motion pictures it was realized that three-dimensional objects could be animated just as drawn and painted characters were. If a puppet, for instance, were to be moved a fraction of an inch at a time, and a motion picture camera were to expose a single frame of film for each movement, the puppet would appear to move when the film was projected. This is called "stop-motion animation," "3-D animation," "dimensional animation," or "displacement animation."

There are several ways in which this can be done. One is a technique called "replacement animation." This was employed by

Pioneer stop-motion effects animator George Pal is seen here with the hundreds of individual figures needed to animate a single character in one of his short "Puppetoon" films. Instead of using a single flexible figure—such as that used in King Kong—Pal created a separate, individual sculpture for each movement. Although this was extremely time-consuming, it allowed for very precise movements and realistic facial expressions. This technique is called replacement animation because the figure in each frame is replaced by a new figure for the next frame.

George Pal in the creation of his Puppetoons and by Henry Selick in the making of *The Nightmare Before Christmas* (1993). Replacement animation requires a separate puppet for every change in pose—or, as is usually the case, separate body parts or facial expressions for each change. It is an extremely time-consuming and exacting task, since each separate puppet or body part must precisely match the ones that precede and follow it—except for the necessary change in shape—for the illusion to work. For a complex action, dozens of different models have to be made. It also means that every movement has to be planned far in advance, allowing little to no creative input or spontaneity on the part of the animator. The technique does have its advantages, though, where radical changes in body shape are required or when subtle facial expressions are important. It is also used when repetitive motions are involved—such as running or walking—since one cycle of motion can be repeated as often as necessary.

More common than replacement animation is the technique used by Willis O'Brien, Ray Harryhausen, and most modern 3-D animators. In this case, the puppets are constructed over a skeleton of hinged and pivoted metal parts. The models are then physically moved a fraction of an inch at a time by the animators. This type of animation allows for the creation of very subtle, realistic movements because the animators are so directly involved in creating the movement. Harryhausen, for instance, is famous for being able to give his creatures real personalities in the way they moved.

Occasionally the two methods are combined, as in *The Nightmare Before Christmas*, where the puppets had poseable bodies and replacement animation faces. This allowed the animators to achieve a great deal of realism when the characters spoke and sang.

A flaw in traditional 3-D animation is that the puppet is not moving when a frame is taken. When a motion picture is taken of a live actor walking, the actor is actually moving when each frame of the film is taken. This means that there is going to be a slight blurring of her legs and arms, for instance. This is just as though you were taking an ordinary still photo of someone.

Inside the original King Kong was a steel skeleton. Ball-and-socket joints allowed the animator to pose Kong in any position desired. (Photo courtesy of Bob Burns)

If they are moving, the picture will be blurred, but if they hold as still as possible, the picture will be sharp. This is the critical difference between 3-D animation and live-action cinematography. Projecting a series of sharply focused frames results in movement that looks hard-edged and "jerky." For most fantasy films, this isn't too much of a problem since it merely adds to the sense of unreality. But if a lifelike effect is desired, the jerky quality of traditional stop-motion animation can be very distracting.

Many animators tried different methods to add motion blur to their films. Their methods ranged from those as simple as poking the model with a finger just as the frame was taken so that it wiggled slightly during the exposure, to shooting through a sheet of glass smeared with Vaseline. Today, motion blur is most often achieved using elaborate setups where the model is moved in a very precise and continuous way by means of computerized motors. This was the method pioneered by Phil Tippet and Dennis Muren to create the smooth motion of the tauntaun in *The Empire Strikes Back* (1980).

Puppets for 3-D animation are sometimes made of colored clays, similar to those used in schools. This makes the entire character not only infinitely poseable but capable of any sort of transformation the animator desires. Will Vinton, who coined the term "Claymation" for this kind of work, used clay animation for some remarkable scenes

The creation of a stop-motion puppet begins with preliminary sketches. (Photo courtesy of Max Winston)

The puppet is first sculpted in clay and then molds are taken from the different body parts. These are then cast in foam rubber, with a bendable metal armature inside. This allows the puppet to be positioned by the filmmaker. Sockets on the bottoms of the puppets' feet (below) allow them to be securely fastened to the floor of the miniature set.

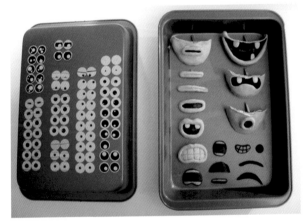

Replacement eyes, mouths, and other features are used on stop-motion puppets.

The stills below (from an amateur stop-motion animated film) show the use of replacement parts to change a character's expression. The basic figure puppet remains unchanged, but features such as the hands, eyes, and mouth can be replaced to make the character appear to move its eyes or open and close its mouth. The puppet of the little girl had ninety replacement eyes to allow her a full range of expression. (Photos courtesy of Max Winston)

Filming a stop-motion movie is a laborious process. The puppets have to be carefully repositioned for every frame of film. Creating just a few seconds of film could take days. (Photo courtesy of Max Winston)

in *Return to Oz* (1985) and his Claymation feature, *The Adventures of Mark Twain* (1985). Nick Park has raised the art to a very high standard in his popular Wallace & Grommet films and the feature-length *Chicken Run* (2000).

Stop-motion animation can be used as an end to itself—as in films like *Chicken Run* or *The Nightmare Before Christmas*—but more often it has to be combined with footage of live actors, so that it will appear as though the actors and animated characters are interacting with one another. There are a number of ways in which this can be done. The puppet can be animated in front of a blue screen and inserted into the live action as a traveling matte. For his fantasy and science-fiction films, Ray Harryhausen developed Dynamation to allow him to shoot his animated characters and prefilmed live action at the same time.

In its most basic form, Dynamation is a variation on the split-screen technique. It consists of a rear projection screen in front of which a stage displays puppet animation. Between this and the camera is a sheet of glass on which is painted a black foreground matte. Prefilmed footage of actors is projected one frame at a time onto the rear screen. The puppet can then be animated to react to the actors.

For example, if the actor is swinging a sword, the puppet can be animated to look as though it were struck by the weapon. During shooting, the foreground matte masks out the part of the live-action frame containing the actor and some of the background. All that the camera records is the puppet in front of the projected background; the rest is blocked out by the matte.

Once the animation is complete, the puppet and its stage are removed from between the rear projection screen and the foreground glass. The film in the camera is rewound to the first frame and the foreground matte is replaced by a countermatte—a second black area that exactly matches the area that had been left clear before—leaving open the original matted out area. The film is then exposed to the lower part of the background image, which had been blocked out before. When developed, the finished footage shows the complete scene with the animated creature included. Done as carefully as Harryhausen did it, the illusion of live actors interacting directly with animated creatures is seamless and totally convincing.

DIGITAL VERSUS DIMENSIONAL

When Steven Spielberg first planned *Jurassic Park* (1993), his intention was to create most of the dinosaurs by means of traditional model animation. Impressive early tests of computer-generated dinosaurs, however, convinced him to use digital dinosaur effects for most of the film. The success of the dinosaurs in *Jurassic Park* in turn convinced a lot of people that traditional 3-D animation was a thing of the past. But just as the prediction that *all* special effects were going to be digital in the future proved to be overzealous, it has turned out that there is still life in the older technique. Many directors prefer the look of 3-D animation and sometimes it is cheaper and easier to produce than a computer-generated effect. Even though the digitally animated dinosaurs of *Jurassic Park* took center stage, dinosaurs in the film were created in numerous ways, each method selected for its final effect in the film. Animatronic puppets were used in many scenes, for instance, as well as a full-sized hydraulically operated Tyrannosaurus rex.

CHAPTER SEVEN
MATTE ART

Matte painting has been one of the oldest special-effects techniques since it was used by landscape photographers long before the invention of motion pictures. The photographers would shoot through large panes of glass suspended in front of their cameras, which would allow them to paint in new details (such as a roof on a building without one) or remove unwanted features. Today, matte paintings are normally accomplished two different ways. The first is

In this example of a matte painting created in the 1940s, the areas in the live action frame that are to be replaced by the artwork have been covered by a black stationary mask (left). This keeps the film in those areas from being exposed. The painted features created by the matte artist then fill in the unexposed black areas of the film (right).

Matte artist David Mattingly working on one of the large matte paintings he created for Dick Tracy (1990). Traditional matte painting such as this is slowly being replaced by mattes painted digitally with programs such as Photoshop. (Photo courtesy of David Mattingly)

the traditional method of combining live-action photography with a painting, the second is creating the painting digitally, then combining it and the live action on the computer.

While matte paintings were originally done on panes of glass and shot simultaneously with the live action, there were so many problems that other techniques soon evolved. One of the more serious problems was that since the matte was shot along with the live action, it was impossible to know if the matte painting was perfectly successful until the film was processed. If there were any problems, then the entire scene had to be redone, which could be an extremely expensive proposition. It was not long before several methods were invented that would allow a matte painting to be safely added to a scene *after* it was shot.

The most common technique employs rear projection. A translucent screen is attached to the back of a sheet of glass and a still frame of the live action is projected onto it from behind. The matte artist, working on the other side of the glass, paints in the area that needs to be replaced, using the projected image as a guide. Being able to work indoors with a still image, the artist can much more accurately match colors, lighting, and perspective than he could if he had to create a matte painting that was to be shot "live." Once the painting is complete, the translucent screen behind the glass is replaced with black velvet. All the live action parts of the painting are now black. The painting is carefully lit and photographed by a motion picture camera. The film is then rewound. The black velvet is removed and replaced by the translucent screen. The lights that illuminated the painting are turned off so that only the projected areas are visible to the camera. The painted areas now appear as black silhouettes, protecting the already exposed image of the matte painting from overexposure. When the film is passed through the camera for the second time, the projected live-action areas fill in the black areas in the previously photographed painting. After the matte painting has been combined with the live-action footage, additional details can be added by double exposure or traveling mattes, such as smoke, flags, lighting effects, and the like.

In one of the final scenes in Titanic, a rescue ship discovers the surviving lifeboats at dawn. The original scene is on the top. On the bottom the matte artist has added the ship, sky, and distant icebergs. (Photos courtesy of Matte World)

A well-done matte painting will look so real that most people don't even realize they've seen one—which is the goal of the matte painter. Matte artist Craig Barron calls it "the invisible art." This realism on the screen is why most people are very surprised when they see a matte painting up close. Instead of a "photo-real-istic" rendering, they see a loose-ly painted impressionistic work, where what appeared to be fine details on the screen are little more than blobs, dabs, and strokes of paint.

More important to a successful matte painting than detail are color, lighting, and perspective, all of which must match the live-action scene exactly. In fact, attention to finicky detail can result in a painting that looks much less real on the screen. Matte painters like to point out that your eye is not really aware of small detail in a real-life scene. It is more aware of color and shape, with your brain filling in the details that it "knows" are there. The matte painter duplicates this by indicating small details with non-descript blobs of paint and brush strokes. When seen from a distance, the result will look very natural.

For The Shadow *(1994), a matte painting was used to transform a California location (above) into a place high in the Himalaya Mountains (below).*

One of the secrets of a successful matte painting is to not crowd the painting with detail (above). It is usually enough to just suggest form and allow the audience to fill in the details in their minds. Many digital matte painters have a tendency to detail their paintings too much. The result is that the finished scene does not look as real as a more loosely rendered, impressionistic one. (Photos courtesy of Matte World)

Three-dimensional objects can also be used in conjunction with a matte painting in order to enhance its believability. In George Pal's *War of the Worlds* (1953), Chesley Bonestell's paintings showing landscapes of Mercury, Mars, Jupiter, and other planets included real rocks and dry ice fog effects in the foregrounds to make the scenes look more realistic.

DIGITAL MATTE PAINTING

Today, most matte "paintings" are created digitally by using software such as Photoshop instead of oil paint on glass. Digital matte paintings can also be created in three dimensions by using software such as Maya or Lightwave, so that scenery and buildings will shift in perspective as the camera moves across a scene, something impossible with traditional matte painting.

Digital matte paintings are created by first scanning each frame of the segment of film that needs to have the matte art added. This transforms the film into a series of digital images. Once they are digital they can be manipulated in any number of ways by a computer, just as you can manipulate a photograph scanned into a computer in your home or school.

The matte artist was able to extend the original scene by adding a painted element to the left side. (Photo courtesy of Pieter Swusten)

This example of a digital matte painting was created entirely using a computer. Many matte painters have been switching from traditional painting techniques to digital ones. (Photo courtesy of Scott McInnes)

The matte painting can be created separately in a program such as Photoshop and then added to the digital scene frame by frame, or it can be painted by the matte artist directly into the scene itself. Working on individual frames also allows the matte artist to add or eliminate small details within the picture. For instance, the director might have overlooked an objectionable sign. Rather than reshoot the scene, the matte artist can simply paint it out of each frame in which it appears. In this way wires suspending models can easily be eliminated. This has made shooting "flying" scenes, where an actor is suspended above the stage floor by wires attached to a harness, much safer. The thinnest possible wires once had to be used so they would not be seen by the camera, but now much heavier, safer ones can be employed.

The pixels that make up the unwanted line . . .

. . . are replaced by pixels between the blue arrows

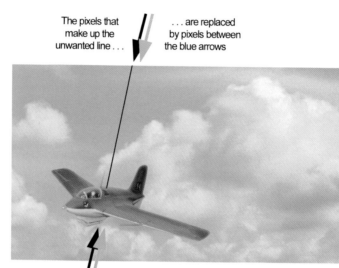

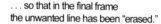

When cables or wires are used to suspend a model or actor they can be removed by a computer. The pixels making up the cables or wires are replaced by pixels from the background. In this way the line is replaced by colors that exactly match the background, and is therefore erased.

. . . so that in the final frame the unwanted line has been "erased."

Among the advantages of digital matte painting is that artists can use real textures and objects by simply copying what they need from reference photos or from a frame of the film itself. If, for example, they need to duplicate a rock texture in a matte painting, artists need only to "cut and paste" the texture from a similar rock in the original frame. This eliminates the old problem of having to laboriously match textures and colors with paint.

If the camera needs to make extensive movements in a shot that includes a digital matte painting, the painting might be created in a 3-D program that allows the artist to create fully sculptural elements. In this way, a building can be added to a scene in which the camera travels completely around and over it.

Today's matte painters can create realistic scenes in part by employing details from photographs of real places. In this example, the artist used portions of the photos at the top to create the finished scene of the castle by the lake. (Photos courtesy of Pieter Swusten)

If there is any drawback to digital matte art is that it occasionally has a tendency to look *too* realistic, falling too often into the problem that traditional matte painters tried to avoid by painting impressionistically and only suggesting details. This gives some digital matte paintings an artificially perfect look that makes them easy to spot. The good digital matte artist will try just as hard as the traditional artist to duplicate a scene the way the eye sees it.

HANGING MINIATURES

One of the major drawbacks to the traditional matte painting was that it had to be used within a very short time during the day, otherwise the lighting and shadows in the painting wouldn't match those in the live-action scene. This problem was solved by the bi-pack contact matte painting and the rear-projection matte painting, which allowed the artist to create the painting after the principal photography had been done, so that lighting, shadows, and colors could be made to match exactly.

Another solution was the invention of the hanging miniature (or "foreground miniature"). Instead of a painting on glass suspended in front of the camera, a small model is used. For example, if only the lower part of a house has been built, the upper part can be filled in by suspending a model of the missing floors at the right distance in front of the camera. If everything lines up properly, the transition from real-life set to miniature model is imperceptible.

The model—which can be part of a building, a ship or other vehicle, a bridge, or a section of landscape—is hung in such a way that its supports are invisible. This is usually done by hang-

By placing a model or miniature near the camera, the illusion that it is much larger can be created. Depth of field is important since both the model and the distance must be in focus.

Camera

Miniature

Support

Live background scene in distance.

Miniature blends with the background when seen by the camera.

Since both the model and the live background scene have the same light source, the lighting matches perfectly.

ing it from above or on rigid supports that extend in from either side. Creating a hanging miniature requires the skills of an expert model maker since the miniature must match the real-life scene exactly.

A disadvantage to the hanging miniature is one that is shared with the traditional matte painting and that is that camera movement is very limited. Should the camera move too much in any direction, the alignment of the model with the live-action scene will change, causing the model to shift and spoil the illusion. But if the camera is pivoted in such a way that it rotates on the nodal point of

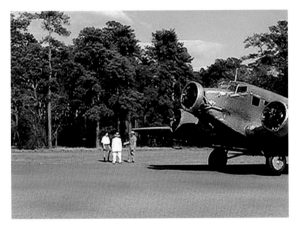

The effect of the actors boarding an old German airplane was created by means of a foreground miniature. The airplane is in reality a commercial plastic model kit obtained from a hobby shop. The filmmaker added small electric motors to make the propellers spin realistically.

It was important to make sure that the surface of the table was covered with material that imitated the look of the real ground in the distance. The model was also shot at a low angle so that it would appear to be the right size.

When the filmmaker looks over the edge of the table, the actual size of the model is revealed, as well as its relationship to the distant actors. (Photos courtesy of Roger Evans)

its lens—the center of the actual frame of film itself—the alignment will not shift as the camera pans from side to side.

There are many advantages to using a hanging miniature. Since it is photographed using the same light as the live-action scene, there is no worry about light and shadows not matching. Parts of the model can be made to move, too, and smoke, fire, and other effects can be added as well. Even though matte art with moving elements and changing light and shadow can now be accomplished digitally, hanging miniatures are still occasionally used since they can have an extremely realistic appearance. Often, too, a skilled modeler can produce a hanging miniature faster and more cheaply than a complex digital matte painting. And since the miniatures are shot "live," directors can make fine adjustments or changes right on the spot. And by looking through the camera's viewfinder, they can

In this scene from a film (above), a spaceship and its launching ramp appear to have been constructed in a parking lot. In reality, they are actually a hanging miniature. The spaceship, launching ramp, part of the parking lot, and several of the cars were all created as a large model (right). When filmed at the proper angle, everything lined up correctly with the full-size scene in the background. (Photos courtesy of Michael Daleo)

see immediately how the scene will look, instead of having to wait until the live action and the digital effect are combined.

FORCED PERSPECTIVE

Related to the hanging miniature are forced perspective shots. These take advantage of the fact that the human eye interprets large objects as being close and small objects as being far away. Not only can a model car or building be made to look full size, human actors can be shrunk or enlarged the same way. The Hobbits in *The Lord of the Rings* (2001–03) are played by full-sized actors. They look smaller than normal because they are actually farther away from the camera than the other actors in the scene. On the other hand, actress Daryl Hanna appeared to be five stories tall in *Attack of the 50 Foot Woman* (1993) by being much closer to the camera than the "normal-sized" actors.

By foreshortening the road in the model (left) the effect of a long road receding into the distance was achieved (bottom). This is an example of forced perspective. (Photos courtesy of Christophe Pattou)

You can use a trick of perspective to take an amazing photo. It is the same technique that makes foreground miniatures and mixed perspective shots like those used in the *Lord of the Rings* trilogy possible.

The secret is very simple: The elf standing on the person's hand in the photo to the right is in fact very far away. All that is necessary to take a photo like this is to be careful to line up the foreground and background objects so that they appear to be touching one another. By doing this, you can make trick photos in which people will seem to be interacting with spaceships, standing on alien landscapes, and many other similar effects. For instance, on page 75, the filmmaker in the photos wanted to show his actors in the same scene with an old German airplane. He purchased a plastic model of the airplane from a hobby shop and fitted it with tiny electric motors so its propellers would spin. The model was then placed on a wooden board that was colored to match the landscape in the distance. When shot

Distant figure appears to be this size

Distant figure on hill

Field of view of camera

Figure standing close to camera

It appears as though the woman is shaking hands with the tiny man she is holding in the palm of her hand. In reality, the man is standing in the distance. By not only carefully lining up the woman's hand, but also making sure that she is looking in the right direction, the illusion is created successfully.

at the right angle, the board blended into the landscape and the distant actors appeared to be standing next to the aircraft.

The actor who is to appear larger or smaller is surrounded by props and scenery made to the appropriate scale and designed to blend in with the corresponding parts of the real-life scene. When shot from the right angle, it is impossible to tell where the miniature or enlarged set ends and the full-size set begins.

CHAPTER EIGHT
OPTICAL EFFECTS

Optical effects are those that are created primarily with the optical printer, though there are many other ways to create them as well. These include effects such as double exposure, split screen, effects animation, stationary matte, traveling matte, and so on.

DOUBLE EXPOSURE

Double exposures are probably the simplest effect to achieve. It involves nothing more complex than shooting a scene, rewinding the film, and then reshooting a different scene. When projected, the finished film shows the two scenes superimposed on top of one another. If the second scene is of an actor dressed like a ghost photographed in front of a black background, the final effect will be the appearance of a translucent "ghost" in the finished film.

SPLIT SCREEN

Another effect that goes back to the dawn of motion-picture special effects is the split screen, which is still effectively used today. In its basic form, it is as simple to accomplish as the double exposure. A black mask—or matte—is placed over the lens of the camera, blocking out a portion of the scene. After the film has run through the camera, it is rewound to the beginning. Now the matte is moved to the other side of the lens and the scene is reshot. The result is two

Running film through a camera twice creates a simple double exposure like the one shown here.

The simple overlapping of two images results in a ghostlike effect.

different scenes on the same film, divided by the matte line. In this way, effects such as having someone talk to themselves can be accomplished. It is also a way to protect an actor from potentially hazardous situations since the actor and the dangerous event can be filmed separately. When actress Ann Francis had to appear with a tiger in *Forbidden Planet* (1956), the scene was shot twice, once with Francis in the scene and no tiger, and a second time with the tiger and no Ann Francis.

EFFECTS ANIMATION

Hand-drawn animation is used to re-create lightning, electrical discharges, beams from ray guns, force fields around spaceships, glowing eyes, flames and sparks, and many other effects. Although most effects animation is added to a film digitally, the actual drawing is usually done by hand.

1. The scene is shot with a stationary matte covering part of the frame

2. The film is rewound and the scene shot again with a counter matte covering the other side of the frame

Using a split screen, the special effects cinematographer can create effects such as an actor portraying her own twin.

3. When the exposed film is developed, the two parts appear together as a single scene

STATIONARY MATTE

Anything that blocks out an area of film so that it won't be exposed to light is called a matte. A stationary matte (or "static matte") is an opaque mask used to block the camera from recording part of a scene. This can be done by something as simple as a piece of black paper or black-painted sheet metal held in front of the lens by a "matte box." This results in part of the film remaining unexposed. After the film is rewound, the original matte is replaced with a corresponding matte—or countermatte—and the new scene is shot. Split screen shots are created in this way.

Another use for a stationary matte might be the insertion of some different element into a scene. For instance, if the screen area of a television set in a scene is masked off by a matte, a picture can be inserted later by means of a countermatte that blocks out everything except for the image that is to appear on the screen.

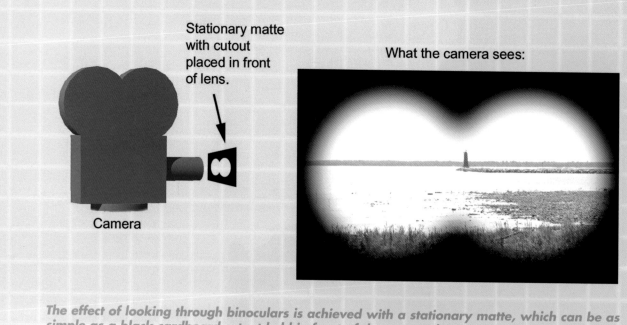

Stationary matte with cutout placed in front of lens.

Camera

What the camera sees:

The effect of looking through binoculars is achieved with a stationary matte, which can be as simple as a black cardboard cutout held in front of the camera lens.

Stationary mattes are also used to create special frames around a scene. For instance, a scene might be framed in the dark figure-eight outline to show what a character is seeing through a pair of binoculars (this is an ancient tradition in filmmaking; the actual view through binoculars is circular). This is done by placing a black card with the required shape cut out of it in front of the lens.

TRAVELING MATTE

Traveling mattes allow directors to insert actors and other elements into a previously filmed scene. If an actor is simply double exposed onto a background, he will look transparent, like a ghost (and this is, in fact, how ghost effects are often created). What is needed is a way to block out the area directly behind the actor, leaving an unexposed actor-shaped "hole" in the film so that when his image is later inserted, there will be no image showing through his body. Since a matte that follows the ever-changing shape of an actor will have to move along with him, it is called a traveling matte.

Over the course of the last century, many different methods of creating traveling mattes have been invented. The basic idea behind the traveling matte works like this: First, the actor is filmed against a backdrop that is a single, continuous color. Filters are used to eliminate this color from the image, leaving the actor surrounded by clear

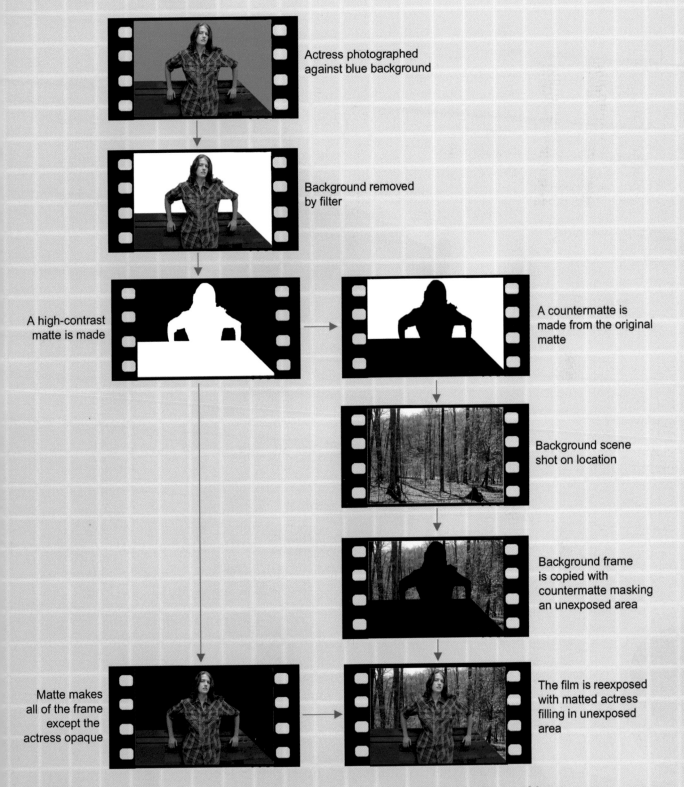

Actress photographed against blue background

Background removed by filter

A high-contrast matte is made

A countermatte is made from the original matte

Background scene shot on location

Background frame is copied with countermatte masking an unexposed area

Matte makes all of the frame except the actress opaque

The film is reexposed with matted actress filling in unexposed area

The traveling matte process allows moving figures and objects to be inserted into a scene.

film. This is called the foreground element. From the foreground element a "female matte" is created in which a solid black area surrounds a clear hole in the shape of the actor. A "male matte," or countermatte, which is just the opposite of the female matte, is a clear film with an opaque, black silhouette of the actor. The male matte is placed over the already-filmed background. When the film is copied, this leaves an unexposed area the same shape as the actor. Then the female matte is placed over the exposed film. The black area shields the background from any further exposure while the clear area allows the image of the actor on the foreground element to be exposed onto the background. When the finished film is processed, the actor will

Make a Traveling Matte

Digital blue-screen compositing works by making a color background transparent so another can be seen through it. You will need to create a uniform, solid-blue background. Seamless blue paper backdrop material can be obtained from a store specializing in photographer's supplies. Illuminating this with blue lights will make it work even better.

Now videotape your actor in front of the blue screen. Make sure the subject is not wearing anything blue as it will also become transparent. The subject should be as far from the screen as is practical to avoid any of the screen color reflecting onto him or her. Good lighting from the side will help to avoid color "spill," too. You will also need to create a videotape of the image you want to use in the background. These two elements could also be a model spaceship and a film clip of stars or an alien planet.

With the two elements completed—the actor in front of the blue screen and the new background—you are ready to composite them into a single image. First, digitize the two shots into your computer by means of a video capture card and then import the video into a commercial digital editing program such as Adobe Premiere or Adobe After Effects. The latter is both inexpensive and popular with students and professionals alike.

In Premiere, the actor you shot in front of the blue screen is placed on the "superimpose" video track, which allows the clip to be made transparent. Then place your background image on the "normal" video track. To make the blue background behind the actor transparent, the video clip is selected and "transparency" chosen appear on the background—exactly filling the hole provided by the male matte—with nothing showing through him.

Most traveling matte systems differ primarily in the colors used for the backdrops and the methods for filtering out that color so that the images can be separated. The green screen system is the one most commonly used today. (Although almost any color can be used, green and blue are the most common since it is easiest to separate human skin tones from these colors.) Although it is highly complex, it allows traveling mattes to be made of delicate things such as hair and of transparent or semitransparent things such as glass, smoke, and water.

from among the video options. When this is selected, a new screen appears allowing you to select the type of "key" required. Select "blue screen." When this is selected, the blue becomes transparent, revealing the new background in its place.

Even though you have accomplished this effect with an ordinary home or school computer, it is exactly the same technique that special effects artists use to place actors in unusual locations or spaceships on another planet.

A model airplane (top) is photographed against a green screen (center). The computer program allows the color to be replaced by any other image desired (bottom). (Photos courtesy of Cristophe Pattou)

When it is not possible to separate an object from its background by means of a color filter—for instance, if the object has been photographed outdoors against a complex backdrop—traveling mattes can be drawn by hand, one frame at a time. This is done by projecting the film onto a special drawing table. The area to be matted is outlined and painted in black on separate cels, one for each frame. These cels are used to create the male and female mattes. Tracing objects from a motion picture film in this way is called rotoscoping. This was most famously done in the Alfred Hitchcock classic, *The Birds* (1963). The director needed to matte hundreds of birds flying over an aerial view of a town. It was impossible to photograph them in front of a blue screen. Footage of birds flying in nature was given to the rotoscope artists, who then laboriously traced every individual bird so they could eventually be separated from their original backgrounds. Two artists needed three months to complete the mattes for the twenty-second scene.

Hand-drawn mattes can also be used to enhance the effect of split screen photography. Normally, a split screen is created by means of a stationary matte placed in front of the camera. Using a hand-drawn matte allows for much more flexibility. In this case the scene is filmed twice, once with the actor on one side of the frame and once with the actor on the other. The rotoscope artist then draws separate mattes for every frame—eventually creating a female matte for one strip of film and a counterpart male matte for the other. These allow the two strips to be combined onto a single strip of film containing both right and left halves of the scene. The advantage of doing it this way is that the matte can move to match the movement of the actor as he walks around the set, allowing him to cross over into an area previously occupied by his other self, something that would be impossible with the unmovable seam created by the stationary matte.

REAR PROJECTION AND FRONT PROJECTION

Rear projection is one of the oldest special effects. It is little more than a translucent screen in front of which actors play out their lines. A film projector behind the screen projects an image onto the screen, creating the illusion that the actors are in some other location. For instance, actors in front of a rear-projected ocean might appear to be on a beach. Rear projection was used (and is still often used) for scenes set in cars, taxis, and trains, where the passing scenery visible through the windows is simply a rear-projected movie. If the scene is set in a location where no movement takes place in the background, a single-frame still picture can be projected.

In order for rear projection to work the camera and projector must be carefully synchronized. If they are not in synch, there would be times when the camera would be photographing a blank screen. This is because both use shutters. A projector is projecting no

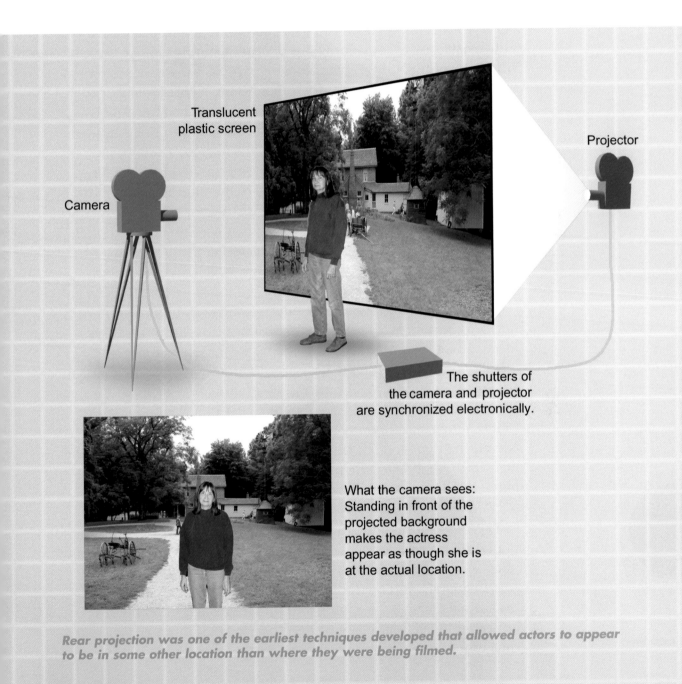

Translucent plastic screen

Projector

Camera

The shutters of the camera and projector are synchronized electronically.

What the camera sees: Standing in front of the projected background makes the actress appear as though she is at the actual location.

Rear projection was one of the earliest techniques developed that allowed actors to appear to be in some other location than where they were being filmed.

image at all between frames, and the camera's lens is closed. By synchronizing the projector and camera—either mechanically by a complex system of gears, or electronically—the cinematographer is assured that every time a frame appears on the screen his camera will be recording it.

Another important factor is brightness. Because the projected image has to be seen on the other side of a screen, it must be very bright. It also has to be bright in order not to be washed out by lighting spilling over from the stage area (though great care is taken not to have any lights shining directly on the screen). Since there is a limit as to how bright an image can be projected without melting the film, technicians sometimes use up to three projectors all projecting the same film simultaneously onto the same screen. This results in an image three times brighter than that produced by a single projector.

Since the background image might be projected to a size anywhere from 100 to 1,000 times the size of the original frame, it is important to use film with the largest frame size possible. This is usually 35mm film. If it is a still image that is being projected, then the largest slide possible is used in order to get the greatest detail and the least film grain. Transparencies as large as 4 by 5 inches (102 by 127 mm) are commonly used.

Great care is taken when creating a background for rear projection—whether it be a motion picture or a still image. Perspective lines and lighting need to match the live-action foreground, for instance. When creating the background footage for a scene that will take place in a car, several cameras are mounted on a special car that is driven along the same route the car in the movie is supposed to follow. One camera points toward the rear, while four others point toward the right and left sides and at 45 degrees to either side of the rear. This way, every angle that might be required during the shooting of the final scene will be covered.

Rear projection was widely used to combine live action footage with miniatures. Willis O'Brien built tiny screens into the miniature landscapes he had built for *King Kong*. By projecting an image of an actor onto the screen from behind, he was able to convincingly combine them with his animated dinosaurs. Like his animals, which were animated one frame at a time, the rear-projected image was also advanced one frame at a time, one for each exposure (otherwise they would appear as a blur in the final film). Rear projection was also a key element in Ray Harryhausen's Dynamation technique.

The main problem with rear projection—and what often gives it away as a trick—is that the image is rarely bright enough to look convincing. This is partly because the image is being seen through a translucent material and partly because the light needed to illuminate the actors washes out the image—much like trying to watch a movie on the big screen with the room lights on. Rear projection often looks exactly like what it is: an image projected on a screen. For *2001: A Space Odyssey* (1968), director Stanley Kubrick introduced a technique that had rarely been used before. Instead of projecting the background onto the back of a translucent screen, he projected it onto the front of an opaque one. This is called, not surprisingly, front projection.

Front projection produced a better image, of course, but there were two huge problems. The first was that stage lights still washed out the image. The second problem was even worse. The actors cast shadows onto the screen. To resolve both of these problems, front projection uses a screen made of a material called Scotchlite. Covered with millions of tiny glass beads, it has the property of reflecting light directly back to its source. It's the same material used for reflective road signs (and the glowing light sabers in *Star Wars*, which were sticks wrapped with Scotchlite).

Kubrick set his actors in front of a Scotchlite screen onto which the background scene was projected. To keep the actors' shadows from being visible, it was necessary that the camera and the projector be on exactly the same line. Since the projector and camera obviously cannot occupy the same space, a beam splitter is used. This is a special type of mirror that reflects only half the light that falls on it. The other half passes right on through. The camera and projector are set at right angles to one another and a beam splitter is placed at a 45 degree angle between them. The image from the projector bounces off the mirror onto the background. The camera, meanwhile, shoots directly through the mirror along the same line as the projected image. The result is that the image on the screen looks extremely bright and clear because the light from the projector is being reflected directly back toward the source, and at the same time the actors cover their own shadows exactly.

In the past, 4-by-5-inch (102-by-127-mm) transparencies were used for front projection, but to get the brightest, sharpest back-

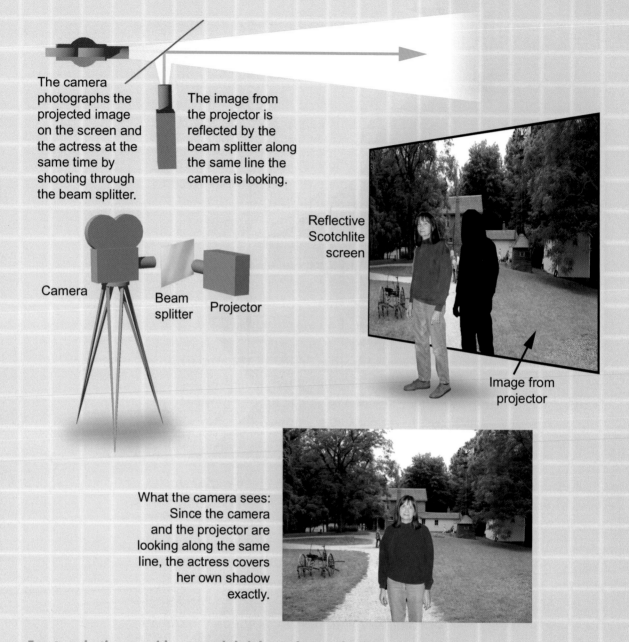

The camera photographs the projected image on the screen and the actress at the same time by shooting through the beam splitter.

The image from the projector is reflected by the beam splitter along the same line the camera is looking.

Camera

Beam splitter

Projector

Reflective Scotchlite screen

Image from projector

What the camera sees: Since the camera and the projector are looking along the same line, the actress covers her own shadow exactly.

Front projection provides a much brighter, sharper background than rear projection.

ground images Kubrick projected 8-by-10-inch (203-by-254-mm) transparencies. This resulted in images of great brilliance, detail, and clarity so that the final scenes in the film look exactly as though they were shot on location instead of inside a studio.

CHAPTER NINE
MAKEUP EFFECTS

Makeup becomes a special effect when it is used to radically alter the appearance or physical attributes of an actor. Lon Chaney (1883–1930) raised special-effects makeup to unprecedented levels when he transformed himself into terrifying creations in the *Phantom of the Opera* (1925) and *The Hunchback of Notre Dame* (1923). To achieve his effects, he relied as much on innovative makeup techniques as he did on his ability to distort his features, sometimes painfully. For example, he gave his face an inhuman skull-like appearance in *Phantom* by distorting his eyes, nose, and mouth with thin wires.

The invention of foam latex appliances in the 1930s allowed actors to radically transform themselves without the necessity of undergoing such painful, and potentially dangerous, procedures. To create new features—or even an entirely new face—with foam latex, the makeup artist first creates a life mask of the actor. The actor's face is covered with plaster. This creates a negative mold of her face. Plaster is then poured into this. After it hardens it is removed and the makeup artist now has a perfect replica, in plaster, of the actor's face. If the film requires makeup to be applied to more than just the face—for example, if an alien creature is being created—a full-body cast will be made. Positive casts are then made from the original negative mold. This positive cast acts as a stand-in for the actor.

Prosthetic makeup can be used for more subtle effects than creating monsters. Here, an actress (top) is made to look much heavier than she really is. On the bottom, one actor has been made to resemble another—in this case, James Earl Jones. (Photos courtesy of Anatomorphex)

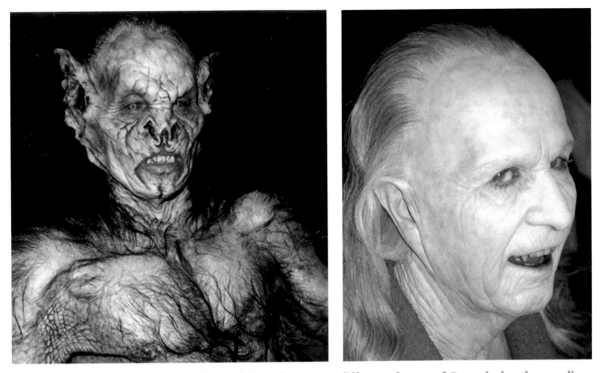

Actor Gary Oldman was transformed into the many different forms of Dracula by the application of elaborate foam prosthetic appliances. The spectacular special makeup effects for Bram Stoker's Dracula (1992) won an Academy Award. (Makeup applied by Matthew Mungle; photos courtesy of Matthew Mungle)

The artist then designs the makeup by applying clay to the life mask or body cast and sculpting it. Once the design of the makeup is finished, another negative plaster mold is made, in the same way that the original life mask was made. When this negative is placed over the original life mask of the actor, there will be gaps where the makeup was. These gaps are filled with liquid latex. The entire mold is placed in an oven and baked. Once the latex has set, the two molds can be separated and the makeup pieces removed. Once they are cleaned up they are ready to be placed on the actor.

If the makeup consists of just a few pieces—a new nose, for example, cheeks, or chin—the makeup artist must make the transition from makeup appliance to the actor's real face blend imperceptibly. Nothing would give away the trick faster than for the audience to be able to see the edges of the appliances. To help hide these, the edges themselves are made as thin as possible. When blended into the actor's face by careful coloring and texturing, the new body parts will then look perfectly natural.

(1) The first step in creating prosthetic makeup is making a life mask or body cast of the actor.

(2) From this mold a plaster replica is made of the actor's head or body. The makeup is created right on the plaster replica.

(3) In the case of this film, Enemy Mine (1985), the complex alien effect required that portions of a mechanical skull be built to allow the face to be expressive.

(1)

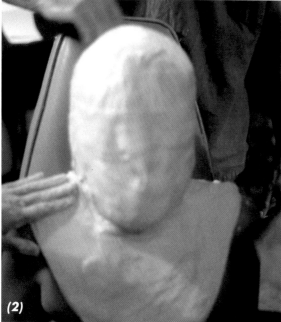

(2)

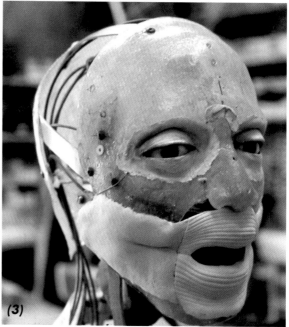

(3)

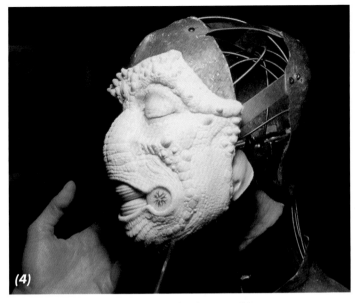

(4) The mask was then applied over this.

(5) And the look is almost complete. (Photos courtesy of Chris Walas)

(4)

(5)

Even when the actor's entire face is to be rebuilt by makeup, it will still be applied in separate pieces instead of as a full face mask. Doing this makes it much easier for the artist to apply the makeup, it is more comfortable for the actor, and it makes the movements of her face look much more natural.

An actor's eyes can be changed almost as easily as any other part of her body. By using contact lenses created by a professional optician, an actor's eyes can be made any color. Even the shape of the pupil can be changed. For instance, an actor playing a catlike creature can be given slit pupils like those of a cat.

DIGITAL MAKEUP

As with virtually every other aspect of special effects, makeup has also undergone a digital revolution. Effects can be created that would be otherwise dangerous or even impossible with traditional effects. Actor Gary Sinise, for instance, played a double amputee in *Forrest Gump* (1994) by having his legs below his knees removed digitally. Arnold Vosloo, in playing the title character in *The Mummy* (1999) and its sequel, was so radically altered by digital effects that not only could pieces of his body be removed, the background could be seen through holes that passed entirely through his face.

Effects that were once extremely complicated and difficult to perform—such as the transformation of a human into a werewolf in *American Werewolf In London* (1981)—can be accomplished digitally. By digitizing the frames containing the actor, they can be manipulated just as for any other digital effect. Animated features can be added—such as Toad's tongue in *X-Men* (2000) or the snakelike arms of the alien Serleena in *Men In Black II* (2002). The mechanical tentacles attached to Doc Ock in *Spider-Man 2* (2004) were also created digitally.

The effect of the mechanical tentacles attached to the back of the Dr. Octopus character in Spider-Man 2 was first conceived as an artist's sketch.

The part of the mechanism that was to appear directly attached to the actor was constructed as an actual appliance. (Photos courtesy of Columbia TriStar Films)

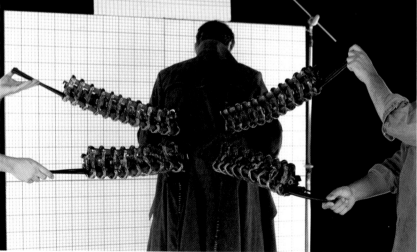

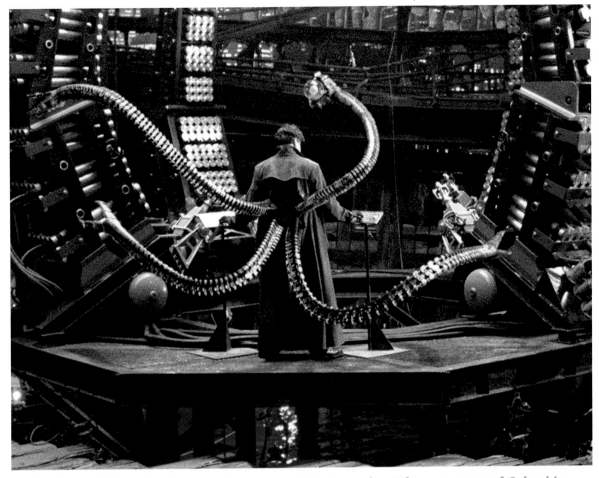

In the finished film, digital animation extended the tentacles. (Photo courtesy of Columbia TriStar Films)

Stage Blood

There have been as many different formulas for making fake blood as there have been makeup and special-effects artists using it. Excellent fake blood (or "stage blood" as it is usually called) can be purchased from makeup suppliers, but it is easy—and less expensive—to make your own. A simple formula that has been used often is a mixture of ordinary corn syrup and red food coloring (enough should be added to make a very dark red color). A few drops of blue food coloring will make the blood look darker and more realistic. Typically, a full ounce (1.0 ml) of red food coloring and about 15 drops (0.75 ml) of blue added to a quart (1.0 liter) of syrup will work fine. Take care: Stage blood will stain anything it touches so it should not be used inside the house or while wearing good clothing!

Entire actors can be created digitally as well. This was done extensively in *Spider-Man* (2002) and its sequel, and in other films such as *Van Helsing* (2004), where real actors were replaced by their digital twins when action was required that would be either physically impossible or too dangerous for a real person to perform.

One character can also be transmuted into another by morphing, an effect used throughout *X-Men* and *X2* (2003) to create the shape-shifting Mystique. Morphing (which comes from the Greek word *metamorphosis,* meaning "to change") involves selecting sets of corresponding points on each image. In morphing one face into another, these points might include eyes, lips, ears, and outline of the head. Based on these sets of points, the computer rearranges the

Most of Spider-Man's incredible stunts in the film Spider-Man 2 were actually "performed" by a digital stand-in that was animated by computer graphics artists. (Photo courtesy of Columbia TriStar Films)

An object (such as a human face) can be transformed or morphed into something entirely different. Points selected on the original are matched to the equivalent points on the new object.

selected pixels to transform the original image into the second via a series of intermediate images. The more similar the before and after images are, the smoother and more convincing the morph will be. Morphing between two human faces is easier than morphing between a human face and that of, say, an elephant. The first major motion picture to feature the effect was *Willow* (1988). Programs similar to those used for morphing can distort or warp an existing image, so that an actor's face or body can be stretched or distorted like those of an animated cartoon character.

CHAPTER TEN

DIGITAL EFFECTS

Motion picture film is composed of a long strip of transparent plastic covered with a thin coating of light-sensitive material. This material in turn consists of microscopic particles. If the picture is enlarged enough, these particles become visible as a random pattern of speckles. These speckles are called the film's "grain." The creation of a picture is a chemical process that results in permanent changes to the particles that make up the grain. Once the picture is formed it is permanent and there is little that can be done to change it. A digital image is an entirely different matter.

A digital picture, such as one you might see on a computer monitor, is also made of individual "particles." You can see these if you enlarge a computer image enough. You will see that the image is actually composed of thousands of tiny squares, each one a different shade of gray or color. These little squares are called "pixels," which is short for "picture elements." The big difference between pixels and film grain is that the pixel is *not* permanent. It can be any color or shade that the computer artist wants it to be. This is because the pixel is not a chemically changed particle—it is a number in a computer. Every pixel in an image—no matter how large the picture is and no matter how many millions of pixels may be in it—has a number that describes its color. A photo taken by an ordinary camera is permanent, but a photo taken by a digital camera

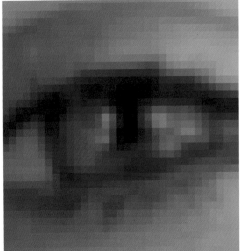

Pixels *is short for "picture elements," the tiny squares of colors and gray tones that make up a digital image. The computer assigns every pixel an individual number, defining its color. If you enlarge a digital image enough, you can see the individual pixels. The more pixels in an image, the sharper and more detailed it will appear.*

can be changed in hundreds of different ways; it can even be changed into an entirely different picture. All the computer artist has to do is change the numbers on the pixels.

Motion pictures are recorded on ordinary film, but this film can then be digitized frame by frame and stored in a computer. This is the same process by which a photograph can be turned into a digital image when it is scanned. Once a movie—or those parts of a movie that need to have digital effects added—has been digitized, the digital effects artist can do almost anything to it she wants in exactly the same way you can change a scanned photograph. Matte paintings, computer-generated 3-D objects, and effects animation can be added; details such as wires can be deleted; and subtle changes to color and other adjustments can be made.

DIGITAL ANIMATION

The digital effect that is probably most familiar is animation. Everything from the dinosaurs of Jurassic Park to the fish in *Finding Nemo* (2003) has been created by means of digital animation.

Computer-generated characters star in *Dragon Fellow*, a student-made film. One of the secrets of a successful CGI character is close attention to detail, such as natural-looking imperfections in textures and colors. These add immeasurably to the believability of the characters. (Photo courtesy of The DAVE School)

Experiment with Digital Animation

You will need: Computer with animation program and paint program

If you have a paint program (such as Photoshop) and an animation program on your computer (many free or shareware programs are available online, such as Tapptoons), you can make an animated movie. Using the painting or drawing program, create a series of simple pictures. Each one should be the same height and width. Number each image file as you do it (for example: 01, 02, 03, and so on) and save them in the format (.gif or .bmp) recommended by the animation program. Each picture

will be a separate frame in your animation. When you are finished, export all of the images into the animation program. The program will allow you to make some fine adjustments, such as the time each frame will be displayed. You can use as many or as few drawings as you like. Often only two or three different drawings are enough to suggest motion. Just as in a professionally animated film, though, the more frames there are the smoother and more realistic the results will be. Instead of animating hand-drawn characters, commercially available programs such as Poser and Strata Pro will allow you to create and animate realistic three-dimensional human figures and objects.

Digital animation shares many of the same characteristics as traditional cel animation or 3-D animation. Every movement is created frame by frame, twenty-four of them for every second of film time. A major advantage that digital animation offers is that the animator does not need to draw and paint every frame, or move the limbs of the animated figure by hand. The computer does all of that work. Digital animation can also take advantage of the ability of the computer to create photo-realistic virtual "models," so that the animated characters can appear as lifelike as the animator wishes.

There are a number of ways in which digital animators can create the figures they work with. A model can be created from scratch, built up in the computer by an artist using 3-D software. This is most often done when the model is of an inanimate object, such as a building or spacecraft. The model can also be created from an actual three-dimensional object. This is most often done when the model is of an animal or human being.

Meticulously created digital animals were combined with live action in this epic scene from Lord of the Rings. (Photo courtesy of New Line Productions)

To do this, a sculptor creates an actual model of the subject. Points are then marked on the surface of the model and lines are drawn connecting them, dividing the surface into a spiderweb-like grid. More points are placed where the most complex animation is to take place and fewer points where there will be not much movement. For instance, the areas around the mouth and eyes on a face will need much more detailed animation than other areas. The animator then records the position of each of these points in three-dimensional space by using a special pen. Since the computer recognizes where the pen is, the surface grid can be digitized, building up a virtual model in the computer's memory. The animator may instead choose to use a device called a cyberscanner. This uses laser beams to measure the three-dimensional position of thousands of points, so that digital models of very complex objects—such as the human body—can be created accurately and very quickly.

Once a model has been created, it is still little more than the equivalent of a hollow shell. This is fine if the model is of an inanimate object like a spaceship, but to duplicate the movements of a living creature—even an entirely imaginary one such as the fish in *Finding Nemo* (2003) or the Gollum in *Lord of the Rings* (2002)—the model needs a skeleton. The purpose of a digital skeleton is the same as that of the armature in traditional 3-D animation. It gives structure and shape to the figure, and it allows the different parts of the body to move in realistic relationship to one another.

The digital animator can take this last characteristic several steps further. By telling the computer to link together different parts of the skeleton so that there is a chain reaction of one part affecting another, extremely natural looking movements can be made very easily. When the animator moves one part of the figure's body, all of the other parts will move in proportion just as they would in nature.

Once the skeleton is created, the next step is to give it "muscles" and "flesh." Muscles are little more than shapes attached to the skeleton that stretch and bulge like real muscles when the figure moves. When the digital "skin" is applied, the movement of the muscles will be visible beneath it, creating a very lifelike appearance. Finally, color and texture are applied to the skin.

The computer can save the digital animator a great deal of time. A traditional animator has to personally move the parts of his model for every frame, but the digital animator can indulge in a timesaving technique similar to that employed by the cel animators

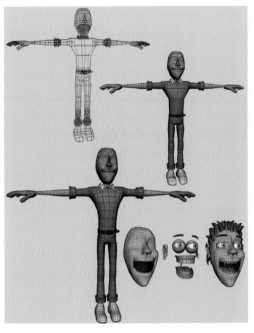

Four of the primary steps in the creation of a digital character are illustrated by animator David Chiu. One of the first steps is creating a wire frame model along with the body parts that will need to move separately—such as the eyes and mouth—and the overall texture or "skin."

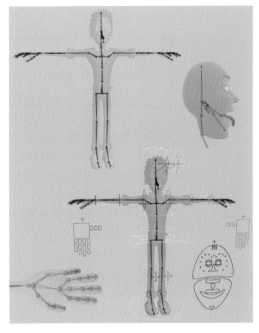

Next, a "skeleton" is created that will allow the character to move. This is the digital equivalent of the armature inside a stop-motion puppet.

The character is then tested, trying out different expressions and movements to make sure everything works properly.

If the animator is happy with how everything looks, he creates the final character rendering. (Photos courtesy of David Urresti Chiu)

who create animated cartoons. When a cartoon is made, the chief animator only creates "key frames" at the most important highlights of the action. An "in-betweener" then fills in the action between the key frames. The digital animator can do something similar. To animate a simple movement, the digital artist might only indicate the beginning and end of the movement—the computer will fill in the frames in between. The more complex a movement is, the more key frames it might require, and for an extremely involved action the animator might personally create every frame.

MOTION CAPTURE

In order to achieve the most realistic movements possible, especially when animating a human being, some digital animators will literally "trace" the movements of an actor. This is done very often in the creation of computer sports games, in which a real-life sports hero will have a digital counterpart who must convincingly move just like the real person. To digitize the movements of a human being a technique appropriately called motion capture is used. The basic idea has

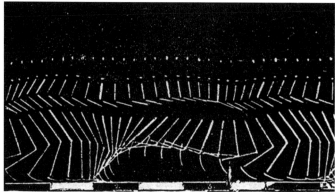

Left to right: The basic principle behind motion capture was established at the end of the nineteenth century as part of experiments in the study of human motion. The subject was dressed entirely in black, with bright white markers at the joints of the body and white lines along the limbs. Then a sequence of photos was taken as the subject moved against a black background. Today, a computer records the changing position of the reflective markers. This record can then be applied to a computer-generated figure, resulting in extremely realistic movements.

been around for a very long time—the first attempts made at the end of the nineteenth century to study human motion used equipment very similar to that of the modern digital effects artist.

A figure dressed from head to foot in black has Ping-Pong balls attached to all the key points of his body: head, shoulders, elbows, knees, and so forth. These are coated with a reflective material. Digital motion picture cameras surround the performer, who then goes through the motions required of the animated character. Since the cameras are at precisely measured fixed positions, the computer can combine the information from them into a single 3-D image that looks something like a white stick figure against a black background. With this data, the digital artist can look at the movement from any angle, finally choosing the one he wants to use. The computer model can then be used as the basis for creating the animated character, which will move exactly as the actor did. The technique results in extremely realistic motions, such as those of the skeletal pirates in *Pirates of the Caribbean* (2003), Gollum in *Lord of the Rings*, and many of the human characters in *The Polar Express* (2004).

Gollum from the Lord of the Rings trilogy was the first attempt at creating a believable, realistic actor entirely through digital animation. Actor Andy Serkis performed all of Gollum's actions, his movements being recorded by motion-capture technology so they could be duplicated by the animators. (Photo courtesy of New Line Productions)

Visual-effects expert Mike Chambers receives many questions from high school and college students who are interested in entering the field of special effects. Here he has put together answers to some of the most important ones.

What classes should I take to get into visual effects and/or the film industry?

A well-rounded education covering a variety of topics is very important. The production of entertainment calls on knowledge from a wide range of subjects, so you shouldn't limit yourself to merely one course of study. On the creative side, consider classes in art, literature, music, theater, cinema, and photography. For technical and practical skills, consider computer science, mathematics, accounting, business, law, engineering, and trade crafts. You may also gain value from courses in history and the social sciences, and in deference to the increasingly global nature of the industry, studying languages is also recommended. Finally (this is important!), regardless of the primary focus of your studies, remember that good communication skills are always required. Writing well and speaking effectively are important to any career path, so the importance of English and composition classes cannot be overstated.

Beyond your studies in school (and watching a lot of movies), you should also dedicate time to personal research regarding the areas of the film industry that interest you. If it is visual effects, then look into the artists and companies that do the work you find exciting. Visit websites and read books or magazines that cover industry subjects, and find out about the latest equipment and techniques. When you have completed your high school education, find a college or university that offers courses focusing on the specialties you would like to pursue.

What schools should I apply to?

Regardless of what discipline you are most interested in, a well-rounded education is always helpful in the film industry. Many universities in the United States and around the world offer very good programs. If you are looking for a more specific education, there are a number of private and community schools that focus on film production, computer graphics, and software education, or fine art–practical art programs. As you will find, there really are a lot of programs to choose from, and I would not say that any one program is more likely to get you working than another. You should contact and visit several schools and determine which one seems to offer the programs and environment that interest you most.

What skills are required?

There are many skills that are specific to certain disciplines that you will pick up over the course of your education and early career. For example, if you are interested in computer effects, then you will need skills in programming and software operation. If you want to be a cinematographer, then skills in photography, lighting, and equipment operation are essential. Needless to say, all the skills needed for every kind of job cannot be listed here, but these will come to you as you pursue your chosen career.

The skills that are most essential, regardless of what you do, are integrity, creativity, dedication, responsibility, flexibility, resilience, patience, willingness to learn, the ability to work well with others, the ability to communicate effectively, and, perhaps most importantly, having a good sense of humor!

How can I gain experience?

Other than education, it is important to start getting work experience. The reasons for this are two-fold. First of all, you will have an opportunity to learn how the business works from the inside. Equally important, however, is that you start making contacts and meeting people who work in the industry. You should look to attain any work experience that you can find, including internships in industry-related fields. You should determine which companies are in your area and start inquiring about entry-level jobs or unpaid internships. In addition to the big visual effects studios that you may have heard about, there are a number of production and post-production facilities around the world (primarily in the bigger cities). Since any experience is good experience, working in a related field or service early in your career can

be useful. (Some ideas might be your local TV or radio station, a local theater or cinema, a professional photography studio, or camera store.) The main thing is to get your foot in the door someplace and start building your resume. Working and meeting people will do as much for your career as does education.

How much does a job in visual effects pay?

There is no one answer to this question. Different jobs pay different rates, and rates will vary depending on many factors, including level of experience, project type and budget, location and term of employment, and whether you are employed on a freelance or staff basis. Needless to say, expect that entry-level jobs will pay low wages, but as you increase your levels of experience and knowledge, work with dedication, and generally make yourself valuable to your employers, you will find that you will be compensated accordingly.

THE FUTURE

Will the computer eventually replace traditional methods of creating special effects? In the excitement of the early years of computer-generated effects, many people thought so. But in the years since, there has been a calmer, more realistic appraisal. It is the ideal machine for compositing images, allowing the director to have unprecedented control over every element in his/her film. It is also a valuable tool for manipulating the final image, allowing the director to touch up even the most minute details.

Most audiences today now assume that every special effect they see on the movie screen is created digitally, much to the annoyance of many special-effects artists. After an initial flurry when directors *did* try to do everything digitally, it was soon realized that even the computer has its limits. It is wonderful at creating some effects and not so good at others. Even some of the elements it creates well are occasionally done just as well by traditional methods—and are often cheaper.

Today's special effects are a healthy mixture of old-fashioned techniques and ultramodern computer technology. Perfect examples can be found throughout the film *Titanic*, which won an Academy Award for its special effects in 1997. Opening scenes showing the great ship docked in Liverpool were done with a flat cutout of a photograph of the ship combined with three-dimensional warehouse buildings and cutout photos of toy trains—a setup worthy of

Georges Mèliés. At sea, the *Titanic* was a combination of a model, digitally animated people, actors inserted via traveling mattes, a digital ocean, and a real-life wake. It is the use of the best of all available techniques—rather than using one to the exclusion of the others—that is making today's special effects so exciting to watch—and so believable.

The possibility of computer-generated actors came even closer to reality with the creation of the perfectly believable Gollum in the *Lord of the Rings* trilogy (2000–2003). The semihuman creature—which was the first fully realized major character in any motion picture to be created entirely digitally—seemed every bit as real as his live-action counterparts. A kind of reversal of this idea was undertaken in *Sky Captain and the World of Tomorrow* (2004), in

Sky Captain and the World of Tomorrow (2004) demonstrated one of the most significant advances in special effects since Jurassic Park. Everything in the film—except the lead actors—was computer generated. (Photo courtesy of © Keith Hamshere/Paramount Pictures/Bureau L. A. Collections/CORBIS)

which virtually everything—sets, props, and scenery—was computer-generated with the exception of the lead actors, who shot all of their scenes against a blue screen.

In the end, it must be kept in mind that in spite of the phrase "computer-generated art," the computer doesn't really create any artwork at all, no more so than the brush the traditional painter uses. It's nothing more than a tool that is only as good as the artist using it.

ACADEMY AWARDS FOR SPECIAL EFFECTS

1939—*The Rains Came*

1940—*The Thief of Bagdad*

1941—*I Wanted Wings*

1942—*Reap the Wild Wind*

1943—*Crash Dive*

1944—*Thirty Seconds Over Tokyo*

1945—*Wonder Man*

1946—*Blithe Spirit*

1947—*Green Dolphin Street*

1948—*Portrait of Jennie*

1949—*Mighty Joe Young*

1950—*Destination Moon*

1951—*When Worlds Collide*

1952—*Plymouth Adventure*

1953—*War of the Worlds*

1954—*20,000 Leagues Under the Sea*

1955—The Bridges at Toko-Ri

1956—The Ten Commandments

1957—The Enemy Below

1958—Tom Thumb

1959—Ben-Hur

1960—The Time Machine

1961—The Guns of Navarone

1962—The Longest Day

1963—Cleopatra

1964—Mary Poppins

1965—Thunderball

1966—Fantastic Voyage

1967—Dr. Dolittle

1968—2001: A Space Odyssey

1969—Marooned

1970—Tora! Tora! Tora!

1971—Bedknobs and Broomsticks

1972—The Poseidon Adventure

1973—(no award)

1974—Earthquake

1975—The Hindenburg

1976—King Kong, Logan's Run

1977—Star Wars

1978—Superman

1979—Alien

1980—The Empire Strikes Back

1981—Raiders of the Lost Ark

1982—E.T. the Extra-Terrestrial

1983—*Return of the Jedi*

1984—*Indiana Jones and the Temple of Doom*

1985—*Cocoon*

1986—*Aliens*

1987—*Innerspace*

1988—*Who Framed Roger Rabbit*

1989—*The Abyss*

1990—*Total Recall*

1991—*Terminator 2: Judgment Day*

1992—*Death Becomes Her*

1993—*Jurassic Park*

1994—*Forrest Gump*

1995—*Babe*

1996—*Independence Day*

1997—*Titanic*

1998—*What Dreams May Come*

1999—*The Matrix*

2000—*Gladiator*

2001—*The Lord of the Rings: The Fellowship of the Ring*

2002—*The Lord of the Rings: The Two Towers*

2003—*The Lord of the Rings: Return of the King*

2004—*Spider-Man 2*

GLOSSARY

Animatronics—Large-scale puppets depicting animals or other creatures that are in large part or entirely operated mechanically.

Aperture—The opening behind the lens of a camera that determines how much light reaches the film.

Armature—The flexible skeleton—made of wire or jointed metal sections—that allows a stop-motion puppet to take on its different poses.

Armorers—Technicians who specialize in weaponry.

Beam-splitter—A prism or special type of mirror that divides the light falling on it into two beams—one in the direction of the original beam and one at right angles.

Bi-pack—The means by which the images on two separate strips of film are combined, or an image from one strip is copied onto another.

Blue screen—A screen or backdrop colored a special blue color. Objects filmed in front of it can easily be separated from the background for the creation of traveling mattes.

Cel—The clear acetate sheets on which individual frames of an animated film are drawn and painted. The name "cel" comes from "celluloid," the material originally used. Cel animation refers to animation created this way.

CGI (computer-generated image)—The application of computer graphics to special effects; also stands for computer-generated imagery.

Cinematography—The art of filming with a motion picture camera. A person operating a motion picture camera is called a *cinematographer*.

Claymation—A stop-motion animation technique that uses figures made of clay that can be molded by hand into different positions between frames.

Cloud tank—A tank filled with water of differing densities used to create cloud effects by injecting colored paint into the water.

Compositing—The act of combining and blending different filmed elements into a single image.

Countermatte—The process of creating composite images. The countermatte has an opaque area where the original matter contains a transparent area. The two mattes are said to be in complement with one another.

Cyberscanner—A device that creates three-dimensional models of objects through the use of laser and video camera. The digital model thus created can then be manipulated by a computer.

Digital animation—Animation created using computer-generated images.

Digital matte painting (*see* Matte painting)

Digitize—The process of turning an image into pixels that can in turn be manipulated by a computer.

Double exposure—Superimposing one image directly on top of another one by running film through a camera twice.

Effects animation—Non-character animation. That is, animation that normally deals with re-creating natural effects, such as lightning, rain, fire and smoke, shadows, etc.

Forced perspective—The process of making objects look farther away than they really are.

Foreground element—An object close to the camera that forms part of the foreground of a scene.

Foreground miniature (*see* Hanging miniature)

Frame—One individual image in a motion picture.

Front projection—The process of projecting a background scene onto a screen from the same direction as the camera.

FX (*see* SFX)

Glass shot (*see* Matte painting)

Hanging miniature—A three-dimensional model that is placed in front of the camera in such a way that it blends with the live-action scene.

In-camera effect—A special effect that is achieved entirely within the camera during the course of original filming. Fades, dissolves, fast and slow motion, double exposures, and split-screen effects are all examples of in-camera effects.

Kinetoscope—An early motion picture projector invented by Thomas Edison.

Matte—A black shape placed in front of the camera lens to block out selected portions of a scene.

Matte painting—A painting that is combined with live-action footage to create a new, composite image.

Miniature—A model of any object made to a reduced scale.

Morphing—The process of changing one shape—such as an actor's face—into another—such as an animal.

Mortar—A small cannonlike gun used to simulate large explosions. An air mortar fires a blast of air that can simulate explosions and other effects.

Motion capture—The process of recording the motion of humans, animals, or other objects so that the motion can later be applied to computer-animated characters.

Multiple exposure—Two or more exposures taken on the same frame of film.

Nodal point—The center of a camera lens.

Pixels—Short for "picture elements," the basic unit of a computer image. When a computer image is enlarged enough, the small colored squares that eventually appear are pixels.

Pyrotechnics—The art and science of fireworks and other explosives.

Rear projection—The process of projecting a scene onto the back of a translucent screen so that the actors standing in front of the screen will appear to be in a different location.

Rotoscoping—The process of hand-tracing objects in individual frames of a film so they can be separated from the rest of the picture.

SFX—An abbreviation for "special effects." Sometimes also "FX."

Short-range apparent motion—The illusion of motion created when two objects placed close together—such as a pair of lightbulbs—are alternately blinked on and off.

Split screen—The process of shooting a frame of film twice, first with one part of the frame exposed, then with the other.

Squib—A small explosive devise that is attached to an individual performer or parts of a set for the purpose of giving the illusion of being impacted by a bullet. They are triggered electrically by remote control and give off no smoke.

Stop-motion animation—A technique by which the illusion of motion is imparted to three-dimensional objects by moving them slightly between each frame of film shot.

Substitution shot—Technique by which objects may be made to disappear or transform into other objects by stopping the camera and restarting it after the desired change to the scene has been made.

Surface tension—A property of liquids that tends to prevent the liquid from spreading. In the case of water, it limits the size of water droplets.

Traveling matte—The process of adding an element to a motion picture frame that was not in the original picture. Unlike double exposure, the traveling matte produces an image that is not transparent.

FURTHER READING

BOOKS

Bizony, Piers. *2001: Filming the Future.* London: Aurum Press, 1994.

Netzley, Patricia. *Encyclopedia of Movie Special Effects.* New York: Checkmark Books, 2001.

Pinteau, Pascal. *Special Effects: An Oral History.* New York: Harry N. Abrams, 2005.

Rickitt, Richard. *Special Effects: The History and Technique.* London: Billboard Books, 2000.

Vaz, Mark Cotta, and Craig Barron. *The Invisible Art: The Legends of Matte Painting.* San Francisco, CA: Chronicle Books, 2002.

Weishar, Peter. *The Art of the 3D Computer-Generated Image.* New York: Harry N. Abrams, 2004.

MAGAZINES

American Cinematographer
The American Society of Cinematographers
1782 N. Orange Drive
Hollywood, CA 90028
http://www.theasc.com/magazine/

CFQ: Cinefantastique
PO Box 34425
Los Angeles, CA 90034-0425
http://www.cfq1.metrikmedia.com/

Cinefex
PO Box 20027
Riverside, CA 92516
http://www.cinefex.com/home.html

Filmfax
1320 Oakton Street
Evanston, IL 60202
http://www.filmfax.com/

WEBSITES

Anatomorphex
http://www.anatomorphex.com
The official website of the special-effects studio Anatomorphex

The DAVE School
http://www.daveschool.com
A school specially devoted to teaching digital animation and visual-effects techniques

Florida FX
http://www.floridafx.com/Index/index2.html
A virtual how-to encyclopedia of special-effects techniques

GIF Animation Instructions
http://www.frontiernet.net/~steve_glimpse/animinst.html
How to create your own animated cartoons on your computer

Himani Productions
http://www.himaniproductions.com/HimAnIMain.html
Excellent step-by-step examples of how a special effects scene is created

Mattepainting.org
http://www.mattepainting.org/
A website devoted to matte painters and their craft, including tutorials on creating matte art

Matte World
http://www.matteworld.com
The official website of the special-effects studio Matte World

Renegade Effects
http://www.renegadeeffects.com
The official website of the special-effects studio Renegade Effects

StopMojo
http://www.mondobeyondo.com/projects/stopmojo/
Free stop-motion animation software

StopMotionAnimation.com
http://www.StopMotionAnimation.com
A website devoted to the work of professional and amateur animators and modelmakers

Tapptoons
http://www.tappsplace.freeserve.co.uk/newanimationsoftware.htm
The website for the Tapptoons Line Tester, an excellent freeware animation program

Visual Effects Headquarters
http://www.vfxhq.com/index.html
News covering the entire visual-effects industry

Visual Effects Society
http://www.visualeffectssociety.com
The official website of a professional organization of special-effects artists

INDEX

Page numbers in *italics* refer to illustrations.

PHOTO ACKNOWLEDGMENTS

The images in this book are used with permission of:

Courtesy of Bob Burns, p. 10 (top); © Close Murray/CORBIS SYGMA, p. 35 (top); Courtesy of New Deal Studios, pp. 35 (middle), 42 (top); 50 (top), 50 (middle); COURTESY OF LUCASFILMS LTD., © 2005 Lucasfilms Ltd. & TM. All rights reserved. Used under authorization. Unauthorized duplication is a violation of applicable law, p. 35 (bottom); Courtesy of Anatomorphex, pp. 42 (middle), 42 (bottom); Courtesy of Robert Skotak, p. 50 (bottom); Courtesy of Max Winston, pp. 60 (top), 60 (bottom); Courtesy of Scott McInnes, p. 66 (top); Courtesy of Roger Evans, p. 66 (middle); Courtesy of Michael Daleo, p. 66 (bottom); Courtesy of Christophe Pattou, p. 79 (bottom); Courtesy of Chris Walas, pp. 91 (top), 91 (middle); Courtesy of Columbia TriStar Films, p. 91 (bottom); Courtesy of The DAVE School, p. 100 (top); Courtesy of David Urresti Chiu, p. 100 (middle); Courtesy of New Line Productions, p. 100 (bottom).

Front Cover: © New Line Productions.
Back Cover: © John Ellis (first from left); © Bob Burns (second from left); © Matthew Mungle (third from left); © Scott McInnes (third from right); © Bob Burns (second from right); © Max Winston (first from right).